v010518
pc: 228
ISBN's:
    978-1-944607-03-6 (B&W, CB workbook, Color PDF)
    978-1-944607-04-3 (Color, PB workbook)
    978-1-944607-05-5 (eBook)

Articulate Storyline 3 & 360:
The Essentials

"Skills and Drills" Learning

Kevin Siegel & Kal Hadi

iCONLOGiC
"Skills and Drills" Learning

Contents

iCONLOGiC

"Skills and Drills" Learning

About This Book

This Section Contains Information About:

- The Authors, page v
- Book Conventions, page vi
- Confidence Checks, page vi
- Book and Storyline System Requirements, page vii
- Storyline Projects and Assets (Data Files), page vii
- How Software Updates Affect This Book, page ix
- Contacting IconLogic, page ix

The Authors

Kevin Siegel is the founder and president of IconLogic, Inc. He has written hundreds of step-by-step computer training books on applications such as *Adobe Captivate, Articulate Storyline, Adobe RoboHelp, Adobe Presenter, Adobe Technical Communication Suite, Adobe Dreamweaver, Adobe InDesign, Microsoft Office, Microsoft PowerPoint, QuarkXPress,* and *TechSmith Camtasia.*

Kevin spent five years in the U.S. Coast Guard as an award-winning photojournalist and has three decades experience as a print publisher, technical writer, instructional designer, and eLearning developer. He is a certified technical trainer, a veteran classroom instructor, and a frequent speaker at trade shows and conventions.

Kevin holds multiple certifications from companies such as Adobe, CompTIA, and the International Council for Certified Online Training Professionals (ICCOTP) as a Certified Online Training Professional (COTP). You can reach Kevin at **ksiegel@iconlogic.com**.

Kal Hadi is a Certified Technical Trainer (CTT) and Certified Online Training Professional (COTP) with more than 20 years of experience in computer graphics, imaging, and electronic publishing. Kal is a graduate of the Rochester Institute of Technology Electronic Publishing graduate program. He is also the author of many books and papers in graphics and web publishing including multiple books on Articulate Storyline.

Book Conventions

People learn by doing. With that simple concept in mind, IconLogic books are created by trainers/authors with years of experience training adult learners. Before IconLogic books, our instructors rarely found a book that was perfect for a classroom setting. If the book was beautiful, odds were that the text was too small to read and hard to follow. If the text in a book was the right size, the quality of exercises left something to be desired.

Finally tiring of using inadequate materials, our instructors started teaching without any books at all. Years ago we had many students ask if the in-class instruction came from a book. If so, they said they'd buy the book. That sparked an idea. We asked students—just like you—what they wanted in a training manual. You responded, and that methodology is used in this book and every IconLogic training manual.

This book has been divided into several modules. Because each module builds on lessons learned in a previous module, we recommend that you complete each module in succession. Each module guides you through lessons step-by-step. Here is the lesson key:

❏   instructions for you to follow will look like this

If you are expected to type anything or if something is important, it is set in bold type like this:

❏   type **9** into the text field

When you are asked to press a key on your keyboard, the instruction looks like this:

❏   press [**shift**]

We hope you enjoy the book. If you have any comments or questions, please see page ix for our contact information.

Confidence Checks

As you move through the lessons in this book, you will come across the little guy at the right. He indicates a Confidence Check. Throughout each module, you will be guided through hands-on, step-by-step exercises. But at some point you'll have to fend for yourself. That is where Confidence Checks come in. Please be sure to complete each of the challenges because some exercises build on completed Confidence Checks.

Book and Storyline System Requirements

This book teaches you how to use either Articulate Storyline 360, which is part of Articulate 360 (a collection of programs available from Articulate via a subscription) or Storyline 3 (which is available for purchase as a standalone product). You can download a free 30-day trial of Storyline or purchase the subscription at **https://articulate.com/360**. You can grab a trial version of the Storyline 3 software from **https://articulate.com/p/storyline-3**.

Once you have installed Articulate 360 you'll have access to Storyline 360. Storyline 3 is a standalone application and you can start it just as you would any program on your computer. According to Articulate, here are the system requirements for using Storyline.

Hardware: CPU, 2.0 GHz processor or higher (32-bit or 64-bit). Memory, 2 GB minimum. Available Disk Space, 1 GB minimum. Display, 1,280 x 800 screen resolution or higher. Multimedia, Sound card, microphone, and webcam to record video and/or narration.

Software: Windows 7 (32-bit or 64-bit), Windows 8 (32-bit or 64-bit), or Windows 10 (32-bit or 64-bit). Mac OS X 10.6.8 or later with Parallels Desktop 7 or later or VMware Fusion 4 or later. .NET 4.5.2 or later (gets installed if not present). Adobe Flash Player 10.3 or later.

Backward Compatibility: Storyline 1 and Storyline 2 projects can be upgraded to Storyline 3 or 360. Storyline 3 and 360 projects cannot be opened or edited with older Storyline versions.

Importing Content: Microsoft PowerPoint 2010 or later (32-bit or 64-bit), Articulate Presenter '09, '13, or 360, Articulate Quizmaker '09, '13, or 360, Articulate Engage '09, '13, or 360.

Publishing to Word: Microsoft Word 2010 or later (32-bit or 64-bit).

Translation: Microsoft Word 2010 or later (32-bit or 64-bit).

Storyline Projects and Assets (Data Files)

You're probably chomping at the bit, ready to dive into Storyline and begin creating eLearning content. As you'll learn as you work through this book, all you need to create eLearning lessons on your own is Articulate Storyline and a little imagination. Wait, you'll also need images... and audio files... the list of supporting assets you'll need could go on and on.

If you have never used Storyline before (and this book assumes you have not), you cannot be expected to learn how to use Storyline on the fly as you create projects. Learning by discovery isn't necessarily a bad thing, but it will take (and possibly waste) a lot of time. We've got a better idea. You provide Storyline (the trial version of the software is fine), and we'll provide all of the project files and supporting assets (such as images and audio files) you need. During the following activity, you will download those assets (data files) from the IconLogic server.

Student Activity: Download Data Files

1. Download the student data files necessary to complete the lessons presented in this book.

   ❐ start a web browser and visit the following web address:
   http://www.iconlogic.com/pc
   ❐ click the **Articulate Storyline 3 and 360: The Essentials** link

2. Save the file to your computer. After the file fully downloads, close the web browser.

3. Extract the data files.

   ❐ find the **Storyline360Data** file you just downloaded to your computer
   ❐ double-click the file to execute it (even though the file is an EXE file, no program will be installed on your computer; rather the EXE is a zipped archive containing Storyline project assets known in this book as data files)
   ❐ if presented with a Security Warning dialog box click **Run** or **Yes**

   The WinZip Self Extractor opens.

   ❐ you can **Browse** and **Unzip** the data files anywhere on your computer that you like (**C:** is the default)

WinZip Self-Extractor - Storyline360Data.exe	✕
To unzip all files in Storyline360Data.exe to the specified folder press the Unzip button.	Unzip
	Run WinZip
Unzip to folder:	
[ ] Browse...	Close
☑ Overwrite files without prompting	About
	Help

   Note: If you changed the **Unzip to Folder** location above, note the location so you can find your files quickly.

   ❐ click the **Unzip** button

   You are notified that several files are unzipped.

   ❐ click the **OK** button
   ❐ click the **Close** button (to close the Extractor)

   The data files have been installed on your computer (within a folder named **Storyline360Data**). As you move through the lessons in this book, you will be working with these files. In fact, you open your first Storyline project from this folder during the activity that begins on page 16.

How Software Updates Affect This Book

This book was written specifically to teach you how to use Articulate Storyline 3 (perpetual license version) or 360 (subscription version). Because Storyline 360 is part of a subscription to several tools known collectively as Articulate 360, it is expected that Articulate will update the tools frequently.

Some of the updates will likely be minor (bug fixes) and have little or no impact on the lessons in this book. However, Articulate could make significant changes to the way Storyline interface, even with seemingly minor updates.

Because it is not feasible for us to modify our books for every Articulate update, some instructions you are asked to follow in this book may not match the updated version of Storyline that you are using. For instance, in the trial version of Storyline, a few items mentioned in this book may require an active subscription and not be available. (We make note of these instances in the book as appropriate.) In addition, the placement of some objects (mainly under the **Insert** and **Format** tabs) may move or the icons modified. Nevertheless, you should be able to easily identify the differences between what you see in this book and what you see in the Storyline interface (given that elements remain under the same general categories).

If something on your screen does not match what we show in this book, please visit the Articulate Storyline page on the IconLogic website for possible book updates or errata information (http://www.iconlogic.com/articulate-storyline-360-essentials-workbook.html). Should you get stuck and find no relief on your own (or from our website), feel free to email Kevin or Kal directly for clarification. You can reach Kevin at **ksiegel@iconlogic.com** and Kal at **kal@amananet.com**.

Contacting IconLogic

Web: www.iconlogic.com

Email: info@iconlogic.com

Phone: 410.956.4949

Notes

iCONLOGiC

"Skills and Drills" Learning

Rank Your Skills

Before starting this book, complete the skills assessment on the next page.

Skills Assessment

How This Assessment Works

Ten course objectives for *Articulate Storyline 3 & 360: The Essentials* are listed below. **Before starting the book**, review each objective and rank your skills using the scale next to each objective. A rank of ① means **No Confidence** in the skill. A rank of ⑤ means **Total Confidence**. After you've completed this assessment, work through the entire book. **After finishing the book**, review each objective and rank your skills now that you've completed the book. Most people see dramatic improvements in the second assessment after completing the lessons in this book.

Before-Class Skills Assessment

1. I can redock Storyline's windows.	①	②	③	④	⑤
2. I can add a Trigger to a slide object.	①	②	③	④	⑤
3. I can edit a Slide Master.	①	②	③	④	⑤
4. I can insert a Character.	①	②	③	④	⑤
5. I can create a Conditional Trigger.	①	②	③	④	⑤
6. I can create a Variable.	①	②	③	④	⑤
7. I can insert a Quiz.	①	②	③	④	⑤
8. I can add a Slide Animation.	①	②	③	④	⑤
9. I can record Screen Actions.	①	②	③	④	⑤
10. I can Publish as HTML5/Flash.	①	②	③	④	⑤

After-Class Skills Assessment

1. I can redock Storyline's windows.	①	②	③	④	⑤
2. I can add a Trigger to a slide object.	①	②	③	④	⑤
3. I can edit a Slide Master.	①	②	③	④	⑤
4. I can insert a Character.	①	②	③	④	⑤
5. I can create a Conditional Trigger.	①	②	③	④	⑤
6. I can create a Variable.	①	②	③	④	⑤
7. I can insert a Quiz.	①	②	③	④	⑤
8. I can add a Slide Animation.	①	②	③	④	⑤
9. I can record Screen Actions.	①	②	③	④	⑤
10. I can Publish as HTML5/Flash.	①	②	③	④	⑤

IconLogic, Inc.
www.iconlogic.com

iCONLOGiC

"Skills and Drills" Learning

Preface

In This Module You Will Learn About:

About Articulate 360, Storyline 360, and Storyline 3

Articulate 360 is a suite of Articulate tools that include the following Desktop applications: **Storyline 360** (which, along with Storyline 3, is the focus of this book), **Studio 360** (a suite of eLearning products including **Presenter**, **Engage**, and **Quiz Maker**), **Replay 360** (a screen recording tool useful for making video demos), and **Peek** (a desktop application that let's you record either Mac or PC screens). There are web-based applications as well including: **Rise** (a template based online authoring tool for creating very simple and responsive courses), **Articulate Review** (online based course review process where many can comment and provide feedback). If you're an iPad user, you can also use **Preso** (an iPad application that lets you create and annotate slides, add video and turn to a movie).

Storyline 3 is not part of Articulate 360. The differences between Storyline 3 and 360 are discussed below.

When you start Articulate 360, you see the following application Launcher screen:

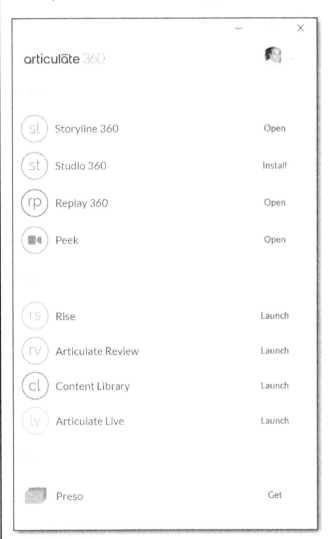

To use any of the tools that comprise Articulate 360, you must subscribe to the suite via Articulate's website. You pay an annual fee of $999 ($599 for the first year if you are an existing Storyline or Studio customer). To edit existing projects, or create new content, you need to keep your subscription active.

In addition to the tools mentioned above, Articulate 360 includes a robust **Content Library** that has a vast array of professional templates and a huge number of characters and other eLearning assets. And there's **Articulate Live**, which provides access to live training events hosted by Articulate.

Articulate Storyline Versions

Introduced in 2012, Articulate Storyline is an eLearning authoring tool you can use to create eLearning courses about *anything*! Need to create an online lesson about terrorism awareness? What about a course on conflict resolution? How about a software simulation teaching colleagues how to attach a file to an email created in Microsoft Outlook? You can use Storyline to create eLearning for all of these... an endless number of subjects. The eLearning content you create with Storyline can be interactive—you can include text, clickable hotspots, quizzes, typing areas, sound effects, videos, audio, and more.

Finished Storyline projects can be published as Flash (SWF), HTML5, and Word documents. The lessons you publish can be posted to Learning Management Systems or web servers, and can be viewed by a learner via desktop computers, laptops, or mobile device such as iPads, iPhones, Androids, Kindles, etc.

During the lessons presented in this book, you will learn how to use Storyline to create both soft skills training (page 30) and software simulations (page 184). Hands-on activities begin in the "Exploring Storyline" module (page 15). Prior to starting the activities, see the "Download Data Files" activity that begins on page viii (in the front section of this book) to download and set up the Storyline 360 data files.

This book covers two very similar versions of Storyline: 3 and 360. As mentioned above, Storyline 360 is part of the subscription to Articulate 360. If you don't want to subscribe to the suite, you can purchase Storyline 3 on its own. Here's a short list of the features you'll see in Storyline 360 that you won't see in Storyline version 3:

- ❏ Articulate 360 Content Library Integration

- ❏ Content Library Templates

- ❏ Content Library Characters

- ❏ More than a million Content Library Photos, Illustrations, Icons, and Videos

- ❏ Integration with Articulate Review for Stakeholder Reviews

If you are still confused about the differences between Storyline 3 and 360, check out this handy chart provided by Articulate: https://articulate.com/360/storyline#compare.

Planning eLearning Projects

By the time you finish the last lesson in this book, you should be able to use Storyline to create some compelling, technically sound eLearning lessons. However, just because you will soon be able to publish technically sound content does not necessarily mean you will go out and create good eLearning lessons. If you want to create good, useful lessons, you have to plan ahead. Before creating a Storyline project, clarify the following:

❑ Why are you creating an eLearning course? You'd be surprised how many people start Storyline and just start creating content. This kind of development process might be well intentioned, but you really need to map out the entire course, including the way you are going to track learner comprehension (if that's important to you). During the mapping process, you might conclude that your course isn't appropriate for eLearning and move on to another course.

❑ Who is your audience? The way you teach children is different from the way you teach adults. For instance, children need praise and encouragement during the learning process; however, an adult learners might find such praise and encouragement annoying.

❑ What exactly are you teaching, and is it appropriate for eLearning? Not every lesson in an instructor-led course can be effectively re-tooled for eLearning. For instance, if a course relies on breakout groups, group discussion, or collaborative work, those aspects of the course cannot easily be included in eLearning. Keep in mind that eLearners almost always work on their own with little or no interaction with a colleague.

❑ Does your project need to accommodate learners with disabilities? If the answer is yes, you should budget approximately 30 percent more time to produce each lesson. Although it's not difficult to create accessible eLearning, it takes more time.

❑ Do you want your projects to contain images and background music? If so, where will you get them? Also, are you going to use a template? If so, who is going to design/create it?

❑ Will there be captions (written instructions and descriptions)? If so, who will write the content for these captions? Do you need an eLearning script? Do you need a voiceover script?

❑ Is your course soft-skills, or is it a software simulation? If it is soft-skills, does it make sense to create most of the content in Microsoft PowerPoint and then import the presentation into Storyline?

Budgeting eLearning Projects

Many new Storyline developers underestimate the time needed to produce projects. Although it is certainly easier and faster to create eLearning content than ever before, it still takes time. To determine your level of effort, the first thing you need to know is the total play time in minutes of your eLearning course. Once you have that number, you can calculate your level of effort.

As an example, let's calculate how long it's going to take you to produce a 60-minute eLearning course. Because you don't want to create a single project that, when published, plays for 60 consecutive minutes, it's ideal to break the 60 minutes of content into chunks. We suggest that each chunk play for no more than five minutes. That means you will have 12, five-minute lessons (or modules).

If you need to write the content for the course (somebody has to), you'll need a script (page 12) and/or storyboard (page 13); and, if there's voiceover audio, you'll need a voiceover script. It could easily take you three hours to write a script to support each five-minute eLearning lesson. Therefore, you should budget at least 36 hours to write the entire one-hour eLearning course (12x3=36). Depending on how fast you write, you could easily double those hours, meaning you may need to budget 80 hours for the writing.

In our experience, writing a voiceover script is easier than writing a step-by-step main script (voiceover scripts typically take us 50 percent less time to write). If you spent 80 hours writing the script, you should budget 40 hours to write the voiceover script. Once the voiceover script is done, you'll also need to include time for recording the audio narration (voice-overs), making corrections to the script post-rehearsal, and recording the simulations using Storyline.

Next comes the production process where you will likely need to add slide text and images (page 53), interactivity (page 79), triggers (page 96), hotspots (page 111), variables (page 115), audio (page 138), animations (page 151), video (page 158), software simulations or demonstrations (page 184), quizzes (page 168), and more. You should budget approximately two hours of labor to produce every single minute of eLearning in Storyline. Therefore, it could easily take 10 hours to produce a five-minute module.

During the production process (detailed beginning on page 6), you'll likely add audio or record audio files (page 138). And you may need to edit the audio files by performing common tasks such as removing unwanted noise (page 141).

When you are done producing the project, you will publish the finished lesson, upload the published assets to a server or Learning Management System, and test for scoring or interactivity errors. If errors are found, you'll need to return to Storyline to fix problems. After fixing those problems, you'll need to republish, repost, and then retest. (You will learn to Publish projects beginning on page 203.)

As an overview, an eLearning development budget for a 60-minute eLearning course might look something like this:

- ❐ 40-80 hours to write an eLearning script or create the storyboard to support 12, five-minute lessons for a one-hour course

- ❐ 120 hours to edit, produce, and test 12, five-minute lessons

- ❐ 20-40 hours to write a voiceover script to be used by your narrator

- ❐ 20-40 hours to record and enhance your own voiceover audio

eLearning Development Phases

The infographic below offers a visual way to think about the eLearning development process and phases. A larger version of the graphic can be downloaded from www.iconlogic.com/skills-drills-workbooks/elearning-resources.html.

eLearning Development Phases

DISCOVERY

Meet with the client. Find out **what they want** in an ideal eLearning course. Who is the **audience**? Define a course **mission statement** for the course in general. You'll also need a mission statement for each lesson in the course. Will the course require **accessibility**? **Audio**? Will it need to be **localized**? What kind of **hardware** will students be using to access the course?

DESIGN

Which tool will you be using to develop the content (**Captivate, PowerPoint, Presenter, Storyline**, or perhaps a combination of a couple tools)? **Instructional design**, a **graphical treatment**, and **navigational choices** are now made and implemented.

WRITING and/or STORYBOARDING

Now that you have chosen a production tool and decided the overall design of the course, you'll need to **plot out the flow** of the course and **write a script and/or a storyboard**. If the course includes voiceover audio, you'll need a separate (and different) script for that.

PRODUCTION

Now it's time to get busy with the **development work** in the selected tool. This includes everything right up to the point of publishing. You'll also **beta test** the lessons in this phase as they are completed.

CLIENT APPROVAL

You're almost there! But, before project completion, you'll need to get your **client's approval**. Depending upon how this goes, **you may need to repeat parts of steps two, three, and four.**

PUBLISHING and IMPLEMENTATION

This includes not only **publishing locally**, but uploading the content to a **web server** or **LMS (SCORM or AICC)**. Be sure to allow time to work out bugs in this phase.

MAINTENANCE

You did a great job! But sometimes changes and updates are necessary. This phase includes **making updates** to the content and **re-posting to the LMS or web server**.

Brought to you by:

iCONLOGiC
www.iconlogic.com

---

eLearning Development Process

We've listed the typical eLearning development process below. The list includes a skill level number indicating the level of difficulty for each task. The numbers range from 1 to 10, with 10 indicating the most difficult task.

- ❒ **Write It:** If you're not a writer, you'll need someone to write the step-by-step instructions (also known as a script or storyboard) necessary to record the project in Storyline. You'll typically find technical writers doing this kind of work, and we consider this the most important process. Without a good script, you don't have a movie. Think we're kidding? The lack of a viable script doomed movie classics such as *Battlefield Earth*, *Barb Wire*, *Heaven's Gate*, *Popeye,* and *Ishtar*. *(Skill Level: 10)*

- ❒ **Rehearse It:** Go through the script with the software you'll be recording in front of you. Don't skip any steps. You'll be able to see if the steps in the script are incomplete or inaccurate before you attempt to record the steps using Storyline. *(Skill Level: 2)*

- ❒ **Reset It:** After rehearsing the steps, be sure to "undo" everything you did. Few things are more frustrating than recording your movie only to find a step you intend to record has already been completed.
(Skill Level: 1)

- ❒ **Record It:** If rehearsals go well, recording the simulation should be easy. *(Skill Level: 2)*

- ❒ **Produce It:** In this task you add captions, highlight boxes, text entry fields, spell check, add buttons, click boxes, animation, question slides, audio, variables, advanced actions, etc. *(Skill Level: 8)*

- ❒ **Publish It:** Although not a difficult task, if your project is large (lots of slides and audio), publishing could take some time. You cannot do any work in Storyline while your project is publishing. *(Skill Level: 1)*

- ❒ **Post It:** This is a broad category. Posting your project means different things depending on where your finished lessons are supposed to go. For instance, if your lessons are supposed to be uploaded into a Learning Management System (LMS), you have to set up the reporting features in Storyline, publish the project, and then upload it into the LMS. Then you need to test the lesson to ensure it scores correctly. If you plan to simply add the lessons to a web server, posting may be as easy as handing the published files off to your webmaster. *(Skill Level: 2 or 3... or higher if your LMS is difficult to use)*

- ❒ **Test It:** This task isn't difficult, but it could take time. If you find a problem, you've got to go back and clean up the project, publish it, and then retest it. Some people argue that this step belongs above the Publish It process. We cannot argue with that logic. However, after testing the project, you still need to publish it, and, as we mentioned above, if you're working with an LMS, upload it and test again. Maybe it should be Test It, Publish It, Test It. See how easy we are? *(Skill Level: 2)*

- ❒ **Republish, Repost, Retest:** If something doesn't work when you test the posted version of your lesson, you have to return to Storyline and fix the problem. After that, you'll Publish, Post, and Test again. Although this may not be a difficult process, it will take time. *(Skill Level: 2 or 3... or higher if you can't resolve the problem)*

Designing Storyline Slides

Because much of the Storyline interface is similar to Microsoft PowerPoint, if you have used PowerPoint, Storyline may seem familiar to you. When working in PowerPoint, you insert slides when you need them and then populate those slides with text, images, animations... just about anything. The same is true when working in Storyline.

There are big difference of course between PowerPoint and Storyline, and you'll discover those differences as you work through this book. What the two programs have in common is your ability to easily create great looking slides and, of course, just as easily create slides that might not look so good. The truth of the matter is that you don't have to be a seasoned designer to produce beautiful and effective PowerPoint or Storyline slides. Toward that goal, here are a few tips to get you started:

❏ There are certain occasions when a bulleted list really is the best way to convey an idea. However, just because PowerPoint uses a bulleted approach to information by default doesn't mean you have to use that format in Storyline.

❏ Try splitting the bullets up into separate slides with a single image to illustrate each point, or forgo the text altogether and replace it with a chart, diagram, or other informative image.

❏ It is not necessary to have every bit of information you cover up on one slide. Encourage your audience to listen and, if necessary, take notes based on what you say, not what is on the slide.

❏ Nothing says "High School Presentation Circa 1997" quite like a dancing animated image clumsily plopped on a rainbow gradient background with a big, garish image (complete with myriad animation effects).

❏ eLearning lessons are plentiful—particularly bad ones. Trust me, your learner will not be impressed with how many moving, colorful parts each slide contains.

❏ Consider taking more of a photographic approach to the images you use. You can easily find stock photographs on the web using any one of a number of pay-for-use websites. There are many free sites, but keep in mind that to save time and frustration (and improve on the selection and quality), you might want to set aside a budget to pay for images.

Fonts and Learning

There is no denying that the most important thing about eLearning is solid content. Read on to discover the many surprising ways fonts can affect your content.

Some Fonts Read Better On-Screen

eCommerce Consultant Dr. Ralph F. Wilson did a study in 2001 to determine if serif fonts (fonts with little lines on the tops and bottoms of characters such as Times New Roman) or sans serif fonts (those without lines, such as Arial) were more suited to being read on computer monitors. His study concluded that although Times New Roman is easily read in printed materials, the lower resolution of monitors (72 dots per inch (dpi) versus 180 dpi or higher) makes it much more difficult to read in digital format. Arial 12 pt was pitted against Times New Roman 12 pt with respondents finding the sans serif Arial font more readable at a rate of 2-to-1.

Lorem ipsum frangali puttuto rigali fortuitous confulence magficati alorem. Lorem ipsum frangali puttuto rigali fortuitous confulence magficati alorem.	Lorem ipsum frangali puttuto rigali fortuitous confulence magficati alorem. Lorem ipsum frangali puttuto rigali fortuitous confulence magficati alorem.
Times New Roman 12 pt	Arial 12 pt
520	1123
32%	68%

Source: http://www.wilsonweb.com/wmt6/html-email-fonts.htm

Wilson also tested the readability of Arial versus Verdana on computer screens and found that in font sizes greater than 10 pt, Arial was more readable, whereas Verdana was more readable in font sizes 10 pt and smaller.

So should you stop using Times New Roman in your eLearning lessons? Not completely. For instance, you can still use Times New Roman for text content that is not expected to be skimmed over quickly or read in a hurry.

The Readability of Fonts Affects Participation

A study done at the University of Michigan in 2008 on typecase in instructions found that the ease with which a font in instructional material is read can have an impact on the perceived skill level needed to complete a task.

The study found that if directions are presented in a font that is deemed more difficult to read, "the task will be viewed as being difficult, taking a long time to complete and perhaps, not even worth trying."

The results of the study by Wilson indicate that it is probably not a good idea to present eLearning material, especially to beginners, in a Times New Roman font, as it may make the information seem too difficult to process or overwhelming.

Most Popular Fonts

We polled our "Skills & Drills" newsletter readers and asked which fonts they tended to use in eLearning. Here is a list of the most popular fonts:

- ❏ Verdana
- ❏ Helvetica
- ❏ Arial
- ❏ Calibri
- ❏ Times
- ❏ Palatino
- ❏ Times New Roman
- ❏ Century Schoolbook (for print)

Fonts and Personas

If you are creating eLearning for business professionals, you might want to use a different font in your design than you would if you were creating eLearning for high school students. But what font would you use if you wanted to convey a feeling of happiness? Formality? Cuddliness?

In a study (funded by Microsoft) by A. Dawn Shaikh, Barbara S. Chaparro, and Doug Fox, the perceived personality traits of fonts were categorized. The table below shows the top three fonts for each personality objective.

	Top Three		
Stable	TNR	Arial	Cambria
Flexible	Kristen	Gigi	Rage Italic
Conformist	Courier New	TNR	Arial
Polite	Monotype Corsiva	TNR	Cambria
Mature	TNR	Courier New	Cambria
Formal	TNR	Monotype Corsiva	Georgia
Assertive	**Impact**	**Rockwell Xbold**	Georgia
Practical	Georgia	TNR	Cambria
Creative	Gigi	Kristen	Rage Italic
Happy	Kristen	Gigi	Comic Sans
Exciting	Gigi	Kristen	Rage Italic
Attractive	Monotype Corsiva	Rage Italic	Gigi
Elegant	Monotype Corsiva	Rage Italic	Gigi
Cuddly	Kristen	Gigi	Comic Sans
Feminine	Gigi	Monotype Corsiva	Kristen
Unstable	Gigi	Kristen	Rage Italic
Rigid	**Impact**	Courier New	Agency FB
Rebel	Gigi	Kristen	Rage Italic
Rude	**Impact**	**Rockwell Xbold**	Agency FB
Youthful	Kristen	Gigi	Comic Sans
Casual	Kristen	Comic Sans	Gigi
Passive	Kristen	Gigi	Comic Sans
Impractical	Gigi	Rage Italic	Kristen
Unimaginative	Courier New	Arial	Consolas
Sad	**Impact**	Courier New	Agency FB
Dull	Courier New	Consolas	Verdana
Unattractive	**Impact**	Courier New	**Rockwell Xbold**
Plain	Courier New	**Impact**	**Rockwell Xbold**
Coarse	**Impact**	**Rockwell Xbold**	Courier New
Masculine	**Impact**	**Rockwell Xbold**	Courier New

Source: Img Src: http://usabilitynews.org/perception-of-fonts-perceived-personality-traits-and-uses/

Scripts

When we have created text-based eLearning scripts or received them from clients, we've generally seen them in two flavors: paragraphs and tables.

Scripts in Paragraph Format

If you are creating a script for eLearning, your text should be formatted in a way that is easy to follow. You can format the script in paragraphs, but you will need to clearly label the parts. You may find that formatted paragraphs are all you need. However, we recommend a table or grid format for a script that will be developed into eLearning.

Step 1

Screen: Display the document

Action: Move the cursor to the Format menu and click Format

Caption: Click Format

Voiceover: Now let's open the Format menu to get started with formatting the document.

Scripts in Table Format

Below is a picture of a script used to create an eLearning lesson. The script was created in Microsoft Word and is available in the Storyline360Data folder (the file is called **SampleScript**).

ICONLOGIC

3320 Breckenridge Way
Riva, MD 21140
410.956.4949 | Fax: 443.782.2366

Sample Script for Recording Screen Actions with Storyline

Lesson Name: Print a NotePad File with Landscape Orientation

Step	Screen	Action to be Taken by Storyline Developer	Caption Text	Narrator Says
1)	A NotePad file should be open prior to recording. You can start NotePad by choose Start > Run and typing notepad. Any open NotePad document can be used for this simulation.	Pull a screen shot of the NotePad file do not click anything. This slide will contain some introductory narrative.	During this lesson you will learn how to print a NotePad document	During this lesson you will learn how to print a NotePad document in Landscape Orientation.
2)	A NotePad file is open. Nothing should be selected and no menus should be open.	Click the **File** menu	First, let's display the Print dialog box. Choose **File > Print**.	To begin, let's display the Print dialog box by choosing the Print command from the File menu.

Storyboarding for Soft Skills

When the training objective is a soft skill, such as how to interact with others in the workplace, or how to comply with legally required behavior, there may be no step-by-step process to spell out. Instead, you have to describe and demonstrate the behavior in a way that engages the learner. This is where the screen-writing part of writing training materials comes into play.

You can present soft skills through slides or videos. Either way, the material must be both clear and engaging.

Here is a typical plot-line for soft skills training.

- ❐ State a real-world problem, challenge, or requirement

- ❐ Illustrate what happens on failure

- ❐ Demonstrate and describe how to succeed

- ❐ Include a quiz or other evaluation

A storyboard, which can be made up of images, text, or both, allows you to plan what is pictured or acted out, as well as what is said for each slide or scene. Even if you are not an artist, you can sketch the basics of the characters, setting, and behavior for each scene. In fact, take a look at the image below. We think that you will agree that the image is not a work of art. Nevertheless, you can tell that it depicts two people meeting in the reception area of an office.

Slide/ Scene No.	Picture	Voiceover	Action	Dialogue
1				
2	*Recept.*			
3	*Rece*			

During the lessons presented in this book, you'll create a soft skills eLearning project (beginning on page 30) that will help consumers lower their credit score. Along the way you'll open and re-purpose content located within a storyboard named **Credit-Score-Coach-Storyboards.doc**. (The file is in the Storyline360Data folder, and you can review it anytime you like.)

Notes

Module 1: Exploring Storyline

In This Module You Will Learn About:

- The Storyline Interface, page 16
- Previewing, page 25

And You Will Learn To:

- Explore a Finished Storyline Project, page 16
- Explore Slides and Panels, page 19
- Zoom and Magnify, page 21
- Explore Panels, page 23
- Preview the Entire Project, page 25

The Storyline Interface

As you work through the lessons in this book, the goal is to get you comfortable with each specific Storyline area or feature before proceeding. Like any feature-rich program, mastering Storyline is going to be a marathon, not a sprint. Soon enough you'll be in full stride, creating awesome eLearning content using Storyline. But before the run comes the warm up. During these first few activities, you will familiarize yourself with Storyline's user interface. Specifically, you'll be instructed to start Storyline, open an existing project, and poke around Storyline's interface a bit.

Student Activity: Explore a Finished Storyline Project

1. Start Articulate 360. (If you are using Storyline 3, skip this step and move to the next one.)

   The process of starting a program varies slightly from one version of Windows to another. We will leave it to you to start either Articulate 360 using any technique you are comfortable with. If you start Articulate 360, your screen will look like the image below.

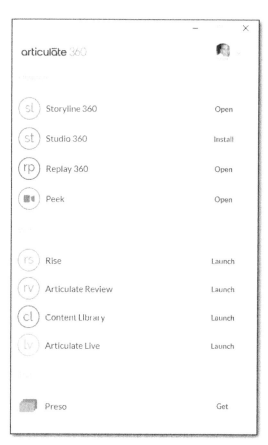

2. Start Storyline 360 or 3.

   ❏ if you are using Articulate 360, on the application **Launcher**, click
   Storyline 360; if you are using **Storyline 3**, start the program like you
   would any program on your computer

   Shown below are the initial screens you'll see when you start Storyline 360
   (the first image) or Storyline 3. You'll notice that the screens are similar. At
   the top left are quick links to start a new project, record the screen, and
   import content from other sources. If you've opened existing Storyline
   projects, those projects will be available in the **Recent** area. Beneath the
   Recent projects, you'll find a **Browse for more** link that will let you find and
   open existing Storyline projects (you'll be using that link next).

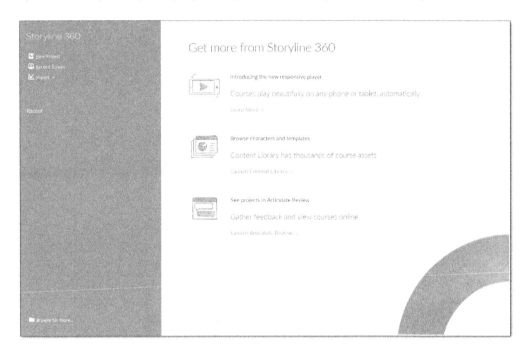

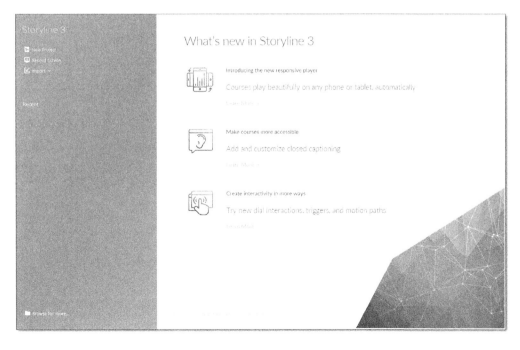

Note: You can open Storyline 3 projects in Storyline 360 and vice versa. If you have not yet downloaded and installed the Storyline360Data files that support the lessons in this book, turn to the **About This Book Section** and complete the "Download Data Files" activity that begins on page viii, before moving on to the next step.

3. Open a project from the Storyline360Data folder.

❏ at the left of the screen, click **Browse for more**

The **Open** dialog box appears.

❏ navigate to the **Storyline360Data** folder and open **Finished_CreditScore_eCoach.story**

The project opens. During the lessons presented in this book, you will learn how to create this eLearning course from scratch. (It teaches best practices for lowering a person's credit score.)

4. Close the project and reopen it using the Recent area.

❏ choose **File > Close** (do not save the project if prompted)

❏ from the **Recent** area, click **Finished_CreditScore_eCoach**

By default, Storyline projects open in Story View. Your screen should look like the image below.

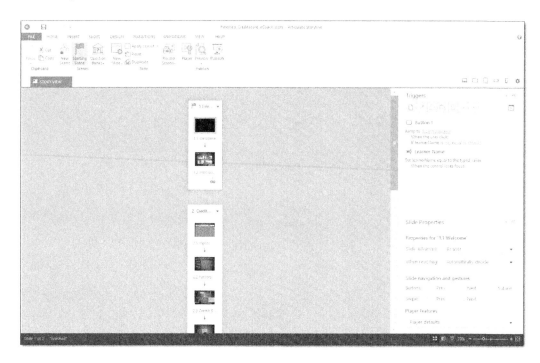

Student Activity: Explore Slides and Panels

1. Ensure that the **Finished_CreditScore_eCoach** project is still open.

2. Explore slides and switch scenes.

   ❏ from the middle of the Storyline window, double-click the slide labeled **1.2 Introduction**

   The Storyline window changes from Story View to Slide View. At the left you'll see a list of scenes. In the middle of the screen, the slide you double-clicked is open, and at the right, you'll see some panels with several options.

   ❏ from the left side of the Storyline window, click the **Welcome** slide to open the slide

   This slide doesn't seem like much... it's solid black. In reality, the slide contains a video that you'll see in a bit.

   ❏ from the left side of the Storyline window, click the **Scenes** drop-down menu and choose **2 Credit eCoach**

   This project consists of four scenes, and each scene contains multiple slides. You'll learn more about the relationship between scenes and slides beginning in the next module (when you create your first project from scratch and begin adding content).

Scenes Confidence Check

1. Still working in the Finished_CreditScore_eCoach project, spend a few moments exploring each of the four scenes.

2. As you move from scene to scene, explore each of the slides within those scenes.

3. When finished exploring, close any open slides to return to Story View. (Open slides can be closed via the Close box in the slide's title tab, which is shown below.)

When you're in Story View, your Storyline window should look like this.

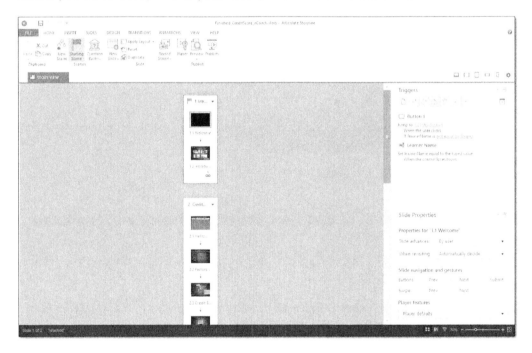

Student Activity: Zoom and Magnify

1. Ensure that the **Finished_CreditScore_eCoach** project is still open.

2. Open a slide.

   ❏ from the middle of the window, double-click the slide labeled **2.3 Credit Score Ladder**

3. Zoom closer to the slide.

   ❏ click the **View** tab on the **Ribbon**

   ❏ from the **Zoom** group, click **Zoom**

The Zoom dialog box opens.

   ❏ select **200%**

   ❏ click the **OK** button

Being this close to the slide makes it easer to view and edit the slide's content and text. At this zoom percent, you will need to use the scroll bars to move around the slide.

4. Change the slide zoom by using the Zoom slider.

   ☐ at the lower right of the Storyline window, drag the zoom slider **left** to zoom out

Note: You can also click the plus and minus signs to change the Zoom.

5. Change the slide zoom to Fit in Window.

   ☐ from the **Zoom** group (on the **View** tab of the **Ribbon**), click **Fit to Window**

Note: You can zoom as far away from a slide as 10 percent and as close as 400 percent.

6. Close the slide.

Student Activity: Explore Panels

1. Ensure that the Finished_CreditScore_eCoach project is still open.

2. Open a slide.

   ☐ from the **Story View** window, scroll down and double-click the slide labeled **3.1 Knowledge Check**

3. Undock the Timeline panel.

   ☐ from the bottom of the Storyline window, drag the word **Timeline** to the middle of the window

   The Timeline panel detaches from the bottom of the window and floats in its own window.

4. Undock the Triggers panel.

   ☐ from the right of the Storyline window, drag the word **Triggers** to the middle of the window

   Now both the Timeline and Trigger panel are detached and floating in their own windows. Using this technique, you can customize the look-and-feel of the Storyline window based on the size of your computer display.

5. Redock all windows.

❐ select the **View** tab on the Ribbon

❐ from the **Show** group, click **Redock All Windows**

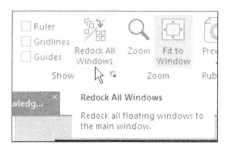

All of the panels return to their default locations.

6. Explore the Timeline panel.

❐ from the bottom of the Storyline window, drag the **Timeline** to the middle of screen

❐ resize the Timeline as necessary to see all of its objects

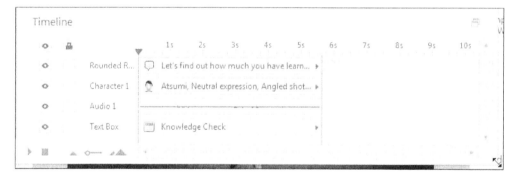

The Timeline appears at the bottom of the Storyline window. You'll be using the Timeline which, among other things, allows you to control when objects appear on the slide, throughout this book.

Panels Confidence Check

1. Still working in the Finished_CreditScore_eCoach project, spend a few moments exploring some of the other panels.

2. Undock some of the panels (position them anywhere you want on your screen).

3. Redock all of the windows.

4. Close the slide.

Previewing

During the activities presented in this book, you will learn how to create the CreditScore_eCoach from scratch. At some point, you will finish the development process by publishing. Once published, the eLearning lesson can be consumed by learners using all kinds of devices (including desktop computers and mobile devices, such as the iPad and the Kindle Fire). Prior to publishing, it's a good idea to preview your project so you can see how the lesson will look once it's published. There are multiple preview options, including Slide, Scene, and Project.

Student Activity: Preview the Entire Project

1. Ensure that the **Finished_CreditScore_eCoach** project is still open.

2. Preview the project.

   ❒ select the **Home** tab on the Ribbon

   ❒ from the **Publish** area, click **Preview** and then choose **Entire Project**

The lesson is generated and then begins to play. All of the slides are interactive to some degree (there are slides with interactive buttons; others contain drag-and-drop interactions).

Note: You can access the Preview tool from any tab on the Ribbon.

3. Preview the Responsive Playback options.

☐ ensure the Preview window is still open

By default, you are previewing the project as a desktop user. However, Storyline projects can be used by learners on several types of devices (such as desktops, tablets, and mobile devices). You can use the Preview window to get an idea of how your content will look on those devices.

☐ from the upper right of the Preview window, click **Tablet Landscape**

Not only does the slide resize to accommodate a Tablet, the Player (which was at the bottom of the Desktop version of the slide) becomes a mobile Player (it's smaller and changes screen position).

Previewing Confidence Check

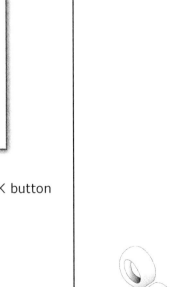

1. Close the Preview window.

2. Select any slide in any scene.

3. Preview the scene.

4. Explore the other Responsive Playback options (Tablet Portrait, Phone Landscape, and Phone Portrait.

5. Close the Preview window when finished.

6. Open any slide in any scene and then Preview the slide.

7. Close the Preview window when finished and then close the slide.

8. Choose **File > Storyline Options**.

9. Here are the default Storyline Options.

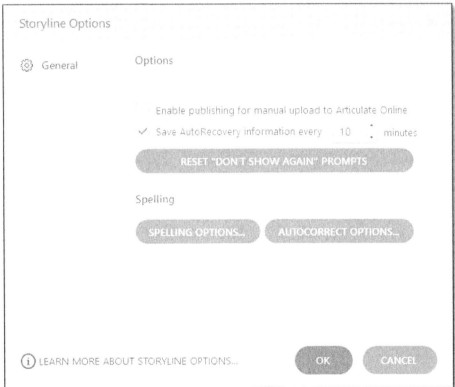

10. Click the **Reset "Don't Show Again Prompts"** button (click the OK button when prompted).

There are several dialog boxes in Storyline that ask you to confirm your action (as shown in the image below). Those dialog boxes will likely contain the option **Don't ask again**. If you accidentally clicked any of the Don't ask again options, resetting the option is a great idea.

11. Click the **Spelling Options** button and, at the bottom of the dialog box, click the **Restore Defaults** button. (The default Spelling options will be selected in the Spelling Options dialog box. Storyline checks for common spelling errors such as double words and case sensitivity.)

Here are the default Spelling Options.

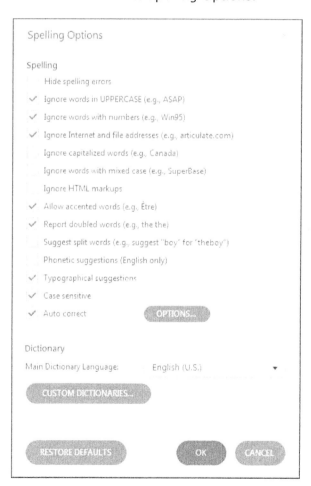

12. Click the **OK** button to close both dialog boxes.

13. Close the project without saving.

iCONLOGiC

"Skills and Drills" Learning

Module 2: Creating Projects

In This Module You Will Learn About:

And You Will Learn To:

Scenes

Scenes are the backbone of any eLearning course you create with Storyline. Every project you create will have at least one scene, but you can create as many scenes as you need. As you create each Storyline project, you should organize each section of your lesson into a separate scene. For example, if you create a lesson that demonstrates a concept and you need a quiz, the demonstration should be created in one scene and the quiz should be created in another. You can easily move the learner between scenes.

The project you are creating will help a user understand how credit scores are calculated. The finished lesson will contain four scenes: Introduction, Credit eCoach, Knowledge Check, and Lightbox.

Student Activity: Create a New Project

1. Ensure Storyline 3 or 360 is running.

2. Use the Welcome screen to create a new project.

   ☐ at the left of the Storyline **Welcome** screen, click **New Project**

A new Storyline project is created. By default, you are taken to **Story View**. There is one scene containing one slide.

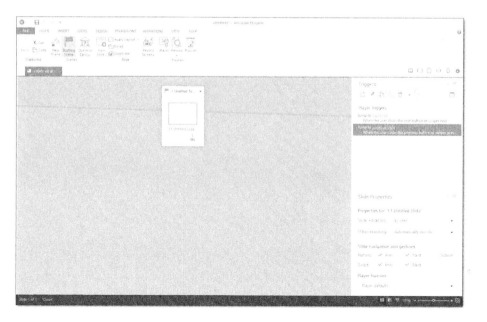

3. Create three more scenes.

  ❑ on the **Ribbon**, select the **Home** tab

  ❑ from the **Scenes** group, click **New Scene**

A second scene is added to Story View at the right of the first scene.

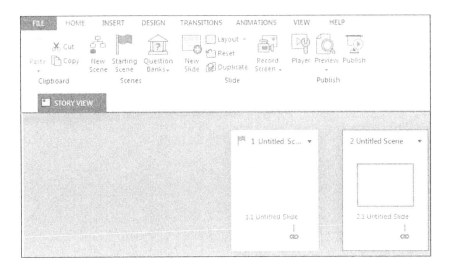

  ❑ on the **Home** tab, **Scenes** group, click **New Scene** again

A third scene is added to Story View.

  ❑ click **New Scene** again

A fourth scene is added. All of the scenes you have added are Untitled. Notice that scene 1 has a red flag in the upper left corner. The red flag indicates the default **Starting Scene** for the lesson. You can assign any scene as the Starting Scene by selecting it and then clicking **Starting Scene** on the Scenes group.

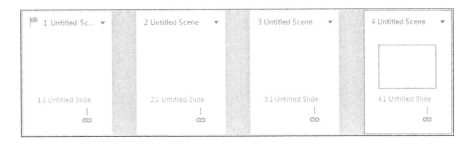

4. Add and delete a scene.

   ❏ on the **Home** tab of the Ribbon, **Scenes** group, click **New Scene**

   You should now have five untitled scenes.

   ❏ right-click the fifth scene and choose **Delete**

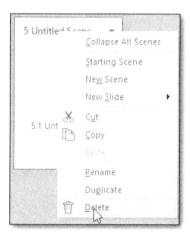

Note: When deleting a scene, ensure that you right-click the scene, not the slide within the scene. If you delete a slide within a scene, the scene is not deleted. Also, you can tell that a scene is selected if there is a thin blue outline around the entire scene.

   ❏ click the **Yes** button

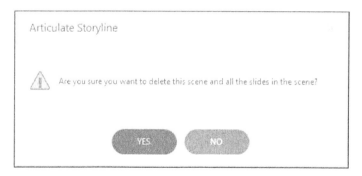

5. Name a scene.

   ❏ double-click the first scene's name (where it says "1 Untitled Scene")
   ❏ replace the existing name with **Introduction** and press [**enter**]

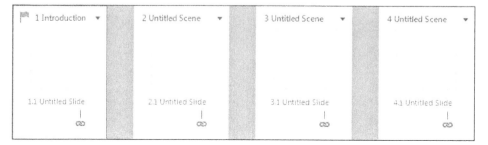

6. Save the Storyline project.

   ☐ choose **File > Save**

   ☐ navigate to the **Storyline360Data** folder

   ☐ name the project **CreditScore_eCoach**

   ☐ click the **Save** button

   The project has been saved to the Storyline360Data folder using the default Storyline file naming convention (the file has a **.story** extension).

Scenes Confidence Check

1. Add a new scene.

2. Delete the new scene.

3. Name for each of the three remaining Untitled Scenes as follows:

   Credit eCoach

   Knowledge Check

   Lightbox

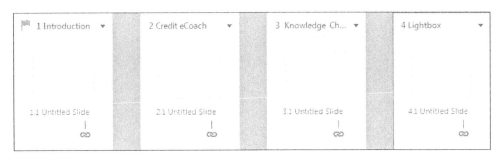

4. Save the project and keep it open for the next activity.

Themes

A Theme is a collection of predesigned and positioned slide elements, master and content slides, styled objects, fonts, and colors designed to quickly give your project a consistent look and feel. Similar to Microsoft PowerPoint, Storyline ships with several Themes that can be applied project-wide in seconds.

Student Activity: Apply a Theme

1. Ensure that the **CreditScore_eCoach** project is still open.

2. Apply the **Brushed** Theme.

   ❏ on the **Ribbon**, select the **Design** tab

   Note that the Themes on the Ribbon are grayed out. You cannot apply a Theme until you select a slide within a scene.

   ❏ select a slide from any scene

   ❏ from the **Themes** group, select the **second** Theme (Brushed)

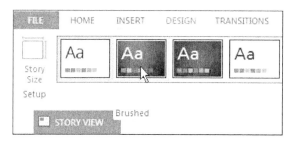

   Notice that every slide in every scene now follows the look of the Brushed Theme.

3. Apply the **Washed** Theme.

   ❏ from the right side of the Themes group, click the drop-down menu

   ❏ select the **Washed** Theme (it's the last one)

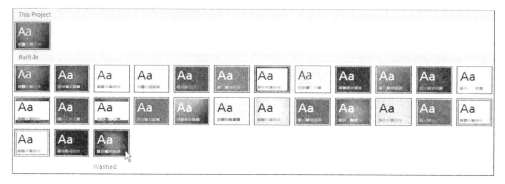

4. Save your work.

Note: As mentioned above, you can apply a Theme very quickly. However, when you switch from one Theme to another, any customization you made to a Theme while working on a project is lost when a new Theme is applied (such as modifying master slides, which you will learn how to do next). It's a best practice to choose a Theme early in the development process to avoid extra work later.

Master Slides

If you need to add common objects to your slides (such as images or background colors), master slides are just the ticket. Each Storyline project Theme contains one Main Master Slide and multiple Content Master Slides (Content Master Slides are considered children of the Main Master Slide).

Instead of manually copying and pasting common objects onto slides, you can add them to a master slide. After that, it's a simple matter of applying a Content Master Slide to selected slides.

Student Activity: Apply a Content Master Slide

1. Ensure that the **CreditScore_eCoach** project is still open.

2. Review the existing slide masters.

   ☐ select the **View** tab on the Ribbon

   ☐ from the **Views** group, click **Slide Master**

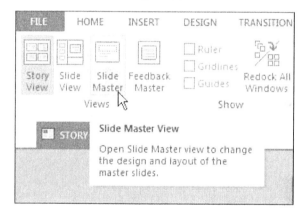

There are six slides at the left of the screen. The top slide is the Main Master slide. The smaller slides are all Content Master Slides. These slides were automatically created when you applied the Theme to the project. Later in this module you will learn how to create a Content Master slide. For now, you'll leave things as they are and use a Content Master on an existing slide.

3. Close the Master View.

   ☐ on the **View** tab of the Ribbon, **Close** group, click **Close Master View**

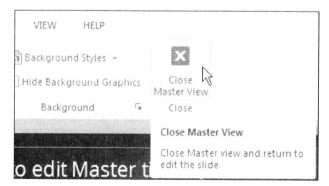

4. Open a slide from within a scene.

   ❒ in the **Introduction** scene, double-click **1.1 Untitled Slide**

   The slide opens in slide view.

5. Assign the Title Only Content Master Slide to a slide.

   ❒ on the **Home** tab of the Ribbon, **Slide** group, click the **Apply Layout** drop-down menu

   The Content Master Slides for the selected Theme appear.

   ❒ select the **Title Only** Content Master

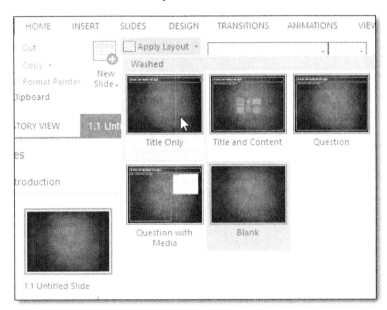

A Title placeholder has been added to the slide.

6. Add a title.

☐ with the Title placeholder selected, type **Introduction**

☐ click away from the placeholder to deselect it

Notice that the text you typed within the Title placeholder has automatically updated the slide title on the Scenes panel.

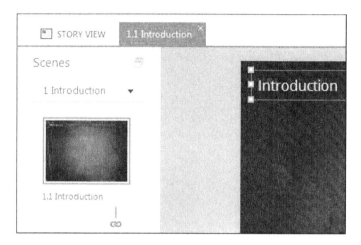

7. Switch to a different scene.

☐ on the Scenes panel, click the drop-down menu and choose the **Credit eCoach** scene

Master Slides Confidence Check

1. Assign the Title Only Content Master Slide to the slide in the eCoach scene.

2. Title the slide **Calculate Your Possible Credit Score Range**.

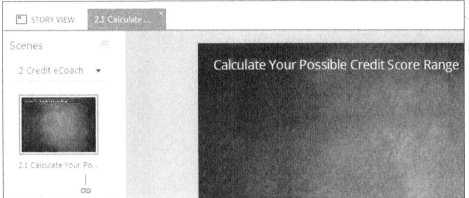

3. Switch to the **Knowledge Check** scene.

4. Assign the **Title Only** Content Master Slide to the untitled slide in the scene.

5. Title the slide **Knowledge Check**.

6. Switch to the **Lightbox** scene.

7. Assign the **Title Only** Content Master Slide to the untitled slide in the scene.

8. Title the slide **Credit Score Estimator**.

9. Close any open slides and return to Story View.

10. Save and close the project.

Content Slides

Content Slides are the backbone of every eLearning project you create in Storyline. The slides you add to your project can be created from scratch in Storyline, imported from other Storyline projects, imported from existing slides created in PowerPoint, or added by recording screen actions (page 184). During the following activity, you'll create slides from scratch. Later (page 48) you'll import content from an existing PowerPoint presentation.

Student Activity: Insert New Slides

1. Open the **SlideMe** project from the Storyline360Data folder.

   Forgotten how to open a project? Look for the **Browse for more** link at the bottom left of the Welcome screen.

   This project is the same project you closed after the last Confidence Check. It contains four scenes, each with a single slide. By default, projects always open in Story View.

2. Insert New Slides.

   ❒ on the **Introduction** scene, open slide **1.1**

   The scene contains a single slide, 1.1 Introduction.

   ❒ on the **Ribbon**, select the **Slides** tab and, in the **Slide** group, click **Basic Layouts**

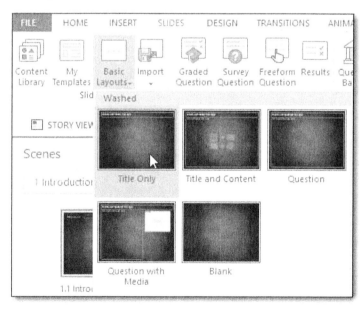

   The Theme being used in the project is **Washed**. There are five Content master slides in the Theme resulting in five different layouts from which to choose.

   ❒ select **Title Only**

   A second untitled slide is added to the Introduction scene.

3. Title the new slide.

   ❏ on the new slide, replace the placeholder text with **Welcome** and then click away from the text

   The title you added appears both on the slide and on the Scenes panel.

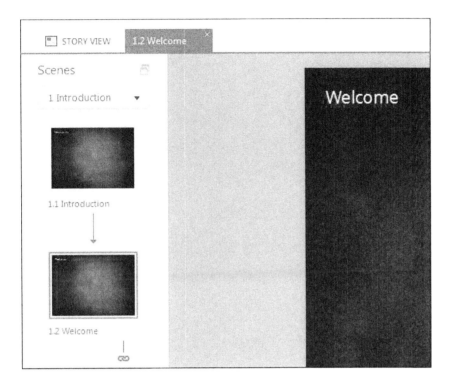

Student Activity: Create a New Content Master Slide

1. Ensure that the **SlideMe** project is still open.

2. Create a new Content Master slide.

   ☐ on the Ribbon, select the **View** tab and then, from the **Views** group, click **Slide Master**

   ☐ on the **Slide Master** tab, **Edit Master** group, click **Insert Layout**

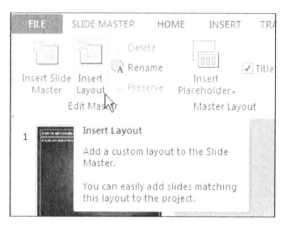

   The new Content Master Slide is added to the list at the left. (It's the **second** slide from the top. If you hover over it, you will see that it's named **Layout 'Custom' used by no slides**.)

3. Insert a Placeholder.

   ☐ on the **Slide Master** tab, **Master Layout** group, click **Insert Placeholder** and choose **Text**

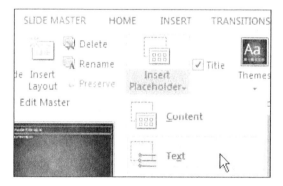

   Notice that your mouse pointer becomes a cross. You can now drag to create a text box.

   ☐ drag/draw a text box that looks similar to the image below

4. Change the text within the Placeholder.

❑ in the new Placeholder, select the words **text styles** and replace them with **subtitle**

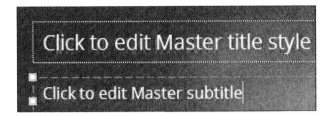

5. Change the text within the subtitle placeholder.

❑ ensure that the subtitle placeholder still selected

❑ on the **Ribbon**, select the **Format** tab

❑ from the **Shape Styles** group, click the drop-down menu (see the image below)

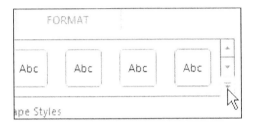

❑ select any shape style you like

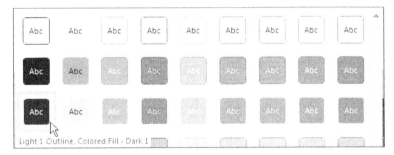

6. Change the border weight of the subtitle placeholder.

❑ with the subtitle placeholder still selected, click the drop-down menu to the right of **Shape Outline**

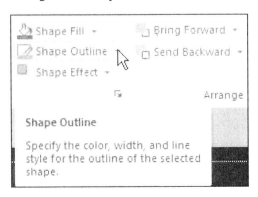

☐ click **Weight** and choose **2 px**

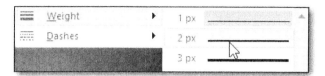

7. Change the vertical alignment of the text in the subtitle placeholder.

   ☐ click the **More Arrow** at the bottom right of **Shape Effect** (pictured below)

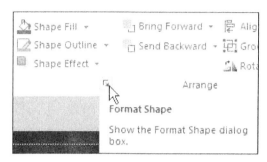

The Format Shape dialog box opens.

   ☐ from the left side of the dialog box, select the **Text Box** category

   ☐ from the **Text** area, **Vertical Alignment** drop-down menu, choose **Middle**

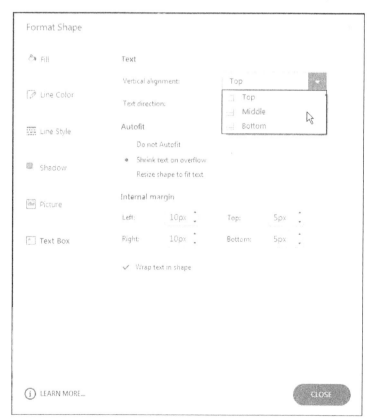

☐ click the **Close** button

8. Change the name of the Content Master Slide.

    ☐ with your new Content Slide Master still selected, click the **Slide Master** tab on the Ribbon and then click **Rename**

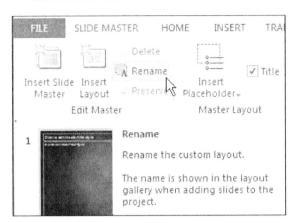

The Rename dialog box opens.

    ☐ change the name to **Title and Subtitle Only**

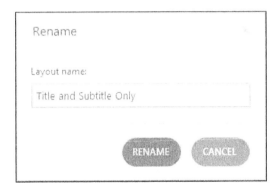

    ☐ click the **Rename** button

9. Leave the Master View.

    ☐ on the **Slide Master** tab, click **Close Master View**

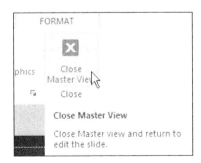

Student Activity: Apply a Different Master Slide Layout to a Slide

1. Ensure that the **SlideMe** project is still open.

2. Apply a different master slide layout to slide 1.2.

   ☐ right-click slide **1.2 Welcome** and choose **Apply Layout > Title and Subtitle Only**

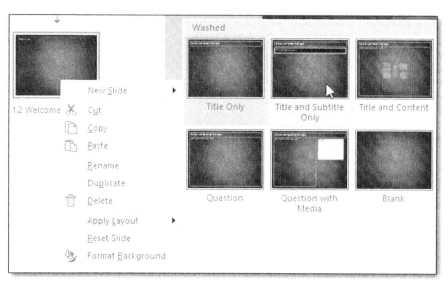

3. Replace the placeholder text.

   ☐ replace the text in the placeholder with **Enter your name and press continue**

4. Close slide 1.2 to return to Story View.

Content Confidence Check

1. Still working in the **SlideMe** project, open slide 2.1. in the Credit eCoach scene.

2. Insert a new slide that uses the **Title and Subtitle Only** layout.

3. Title the new slide **Factors That Affect Your Credit Score**.

4. Add the following subtitle: **You must click every button below before you can continue.**

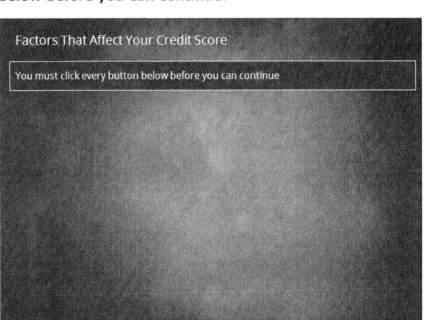

5. Insert another new slide that uses the **Title Only** layout.

6. Title the new slide **Credit Score Estimator**.

7. Close the slide and return to Story View.

8. Save your work. Keep the project open for the next activity.

PowerPoint Integration

If you have already created a presentation using Microsoft PowerPoint and want to use that content for eLearning, there's no need to recreate that content in Storyline. You can import the presentation slides into an existing Storyline project or create a new project that uses the PowerPoint slides. Once you have imported the PowerPoint slides into Storyline, most of the PowerPoint objects can be moved or edited directly within Storyline.

> **Note:** You must have PowerPoint 2007 or newer installed on your computer before you can import PowerPoint content into Storyline.

Student Activity: Import Content From PowerPoint

1. Ensure that the **SlideMe** project is still open.

2. Import a slide from an existing PowerPoint presentation into Storyline.

   ❏ open slide **1.1 Introduction**

   ❏ on the **Ribbon**, click the **Slides** tab

   ❏ from the **Slide** group, click **Import**

   ❏ click **Import PowerPoint**

   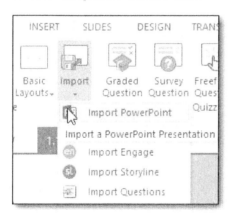

   ❏ from the **Storyline360Data** folder, open **PowerPointContent**

   A preview of the two slides in the PowerPointContent presentation appears. You can always elect to import all of a presentation's slides. Or, as is the case here, you can select a portion of the presentation. (If you receive an error message while trying to import PowerPoint slides, refer to this Articulate support article: http://www.articulate.com/support/storyline/error-failed-to-import-powerpoint-presentation.)

   ❏ at the upper right of the dialog box, click **None**

   ❏ from the **Presentation** area, select only the **Introduction** slide

---

❏ from the **Insert into scene** drop-down menu, choose **Current scene**

❏ click the **Import** button

The selected PowerPoint slide is imported into Storyline.

❏ select slide **1.2 Introduction** (this is the new, imported slide)

Notice that the appearance of the PowerPoint slide does not match your layout. You'll take care of that next.

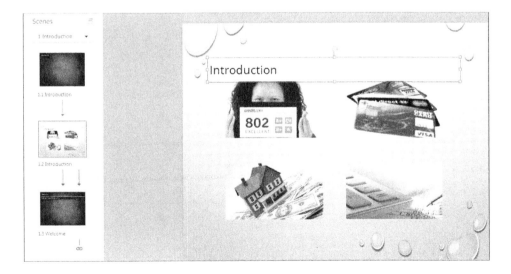

3. Reformat the imported PowerPoint slide.

☐ on the **Scenes** panel, right-click slide **1.2 Introduction** and choose **Apply Layout > Title Only** (from the top of the layouts)

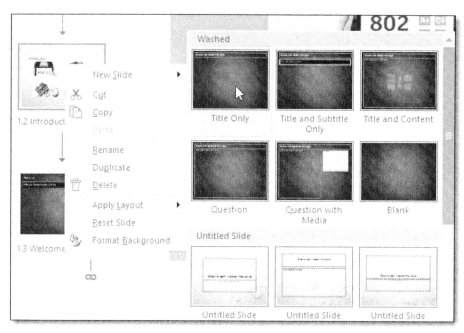

Note: While the slide now looks like a Title Only slide, the font size is a bit smaller than what was used on the master slide. You'll worry about formatting text in the next module.

PowerPoint Confidence Check

1. Still working in the **SlideMe** project, delete slide **1.1 Introduction** (because you've imported the content from PowerPoint, this slide is no longer necessary).

2. Go to the **Master View** (you learned how to work on the Master View beginning on page 36) and delete the slide masters and the layouts that were imported from PowerPoint (those are all of the gray slides—there are a bunch of them).

3. Close the Master View.

4. Close the slide.

5. Save and close the project.

Notes

iCONLOGiC
"Skills and Drills" Learning

Module 3: Add Content

In This Module You Will Learn About:

And You Will Learn To:

Text Boxes

Text can be inserted onto any Storyline slide by typing directly into text boxes, shapes, or captions. You can also copy and paste text from existing sources, such as your favorite word processor, website, or email.

> **Note:** When you paste text into Storyline, you have three paste options: Use Destination Theme, Keep Source Formatting, and Text Only.

Student Activity: Create and Format a Text Box

1. Open the **ContentMe** project from the Storyline360Data folder.

2. Open slide **2.1** (in the Credit eCoach scene).

3. Insert a Text Box and add content to it.

   ❏ select the **Insert** tab on the **Ribbon**

   ❏ from the **Text** group, click **Text Box**

   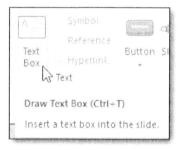

   Your mouse pointer changes appearance and is now a cross. A cross icon indicates that you can draw an object.

   ❏ draw a large box that is **as wide as the slide**

   The height of the box is not important at this time. The box will get taller as you add content.

   ❏ type **The Credit Score Estimator is shown below. You can drag the sliders left or right to help the Estimator calculate your credit score.**

   Calculate Your Possible Credit Score Range

   The Credit Score Estimator is shown below. You can drag the sliders left or right to help the Estimator calculate your credit score.

4. Apply a Shape Style to the text box.

   ❏ with the text box still selected, click the **Format** tab on the **Ribbon**

   ❏ from the **Shape Styles** group, click the drop-down (shown below)

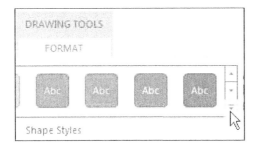

   ❏ select **any** Shape Style that you like

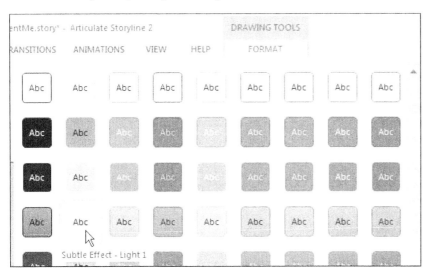

5. Format the text box.

   ❏ right-click the text box and choose **Format Shape**

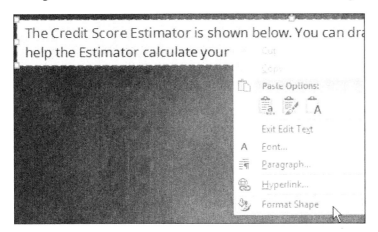

The Format Shape dialog box opens.

❑ from the list at the left, select **Text Box**

❑ from the **Internal margin** area, change the **Top** margin to **10**

❑ change the **Bottom** margin to **10**

❑ click the **Close** button

Notice that extra space has been added to the top and bottom of the text box.

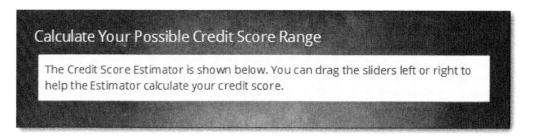

6. Save your work.

Student Activity: Work with a List

1. Copy content from a Word document.

   ❏ start **Microsoft Word**

   ❏ using **Word**, open **Credit-Score-Coach-Storyboards** from the Storyline360Data folder

   ❏ from the **Slide 1.1 section** of the storyboard, select from **In this course, you will learn** through **Ways to improve your credit.**

   > In this course, you will learn:
   >
   > How your credit score is calculated
   >
   > How credit score affects your cost when borrowing for a new home
   >
   > Ways to improve your credit

   ❏ copy the text ([**ctrl**] [**c**] works great)

2. Return to Storyline and ensure that the **ContentMe** project is still open.

3. Paste content from Word into Storyline.

   ❏ close slide **2.1** to return to Story View

   ❏ open slide **1.1** (it's within the **Introduction** scene)

   ❏ right-click the slide and from the **Paste Options** area, choose **Use Destination Theme**

The text is pasted in the middle of the slide and is covering the slide's images. Next you'll hide those images to make it easier to work with the text.

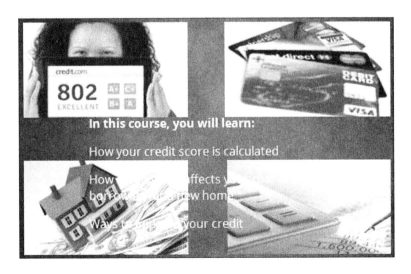

4. Hide slide objects.

❏ on the **Timeline** (located at the bottom of the Storyline window), click the **Show/Hide** tool to the left of Pictures **6**, **5**, **4**, and **3**

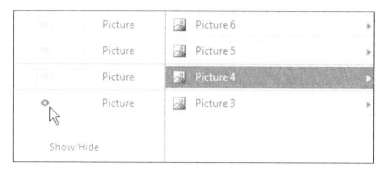

With the images hidden, it's now easier to focus your attention on the slide text.

5. Reformat a list.

❏ click within the text box

❏ select all of the text within the text box except the heading "In this course…"

❏ click the **Home** tab on the **Ribbon**

❏ from the **Paragraph** group, click the drop-down menu to the right of **Bullets**

❏ click the **cubes** bullet

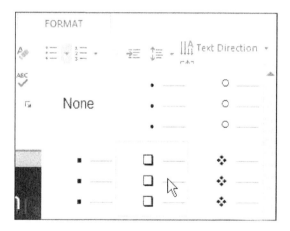

6. Modify the bullet's color to white.

☐ from the **Paragraph** group on the **Home** tab, click the drop-down menu to the right of **Bullets** again and choose **Bullets and Numbering**

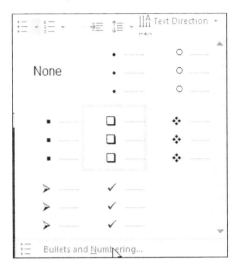

The Bullets and Numbering dialog box opens.

☐ ensure you are working on the **Bulleted** tab

☐ from the bottom left of the dialog box, click the **Color** drop-down menu and choose **White**

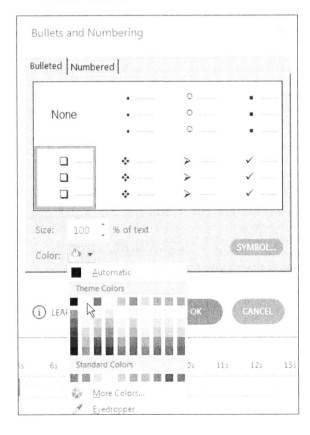

☐ click the **OK** button

7. Change the line spacing of the bulleted list.

❏ on the **Timeline**, click the object with the words "In this course..."

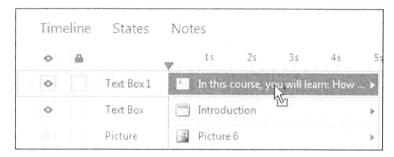

You've selected the text box, but not the content within the box. You can tell if you've selected the box versus its content by the appearance of the object's border. If you had clicked within the text box, the border would have appeared as dashes instead of solid. You're about to change the line spacing for the entire box. Had you selected text within the box, the change you are about to make would have affected only the selection.

❏ from the **Paragraph** group on the **Home** tab, click the **Line Spacing** drop-down menu and choose **Line Spacing Options**

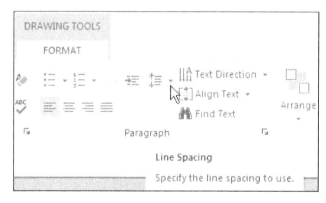

The Paragraph dialog box opens.

❏ from the bottom right of the dialog box, change the **Line Spacing** to **Exactly**

❏ change the **At** to **45**

❏ click the **OK** button

8. Change the size and position of the text box.

☐ right-click the border of the text box and choose **Size and Position**

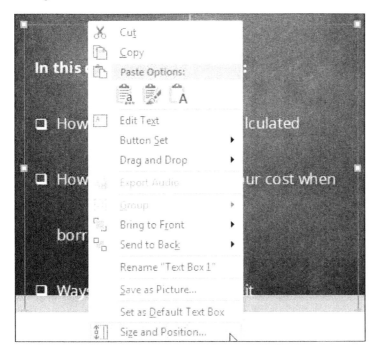

The **Size and Position** dialog box opens.

☐ from the **left** of the dialog box, select **Size**

☐ from the **Size and rotate** area, change the Width to **620**

☐ from the left of the dialog box, select **Position**

☐ from the **Position on slide** area, change the **Horizontal** to **75**

☐ change the **Vertical** to **100**

☐ click the **Close** button

Your slide should look similar to the image below.

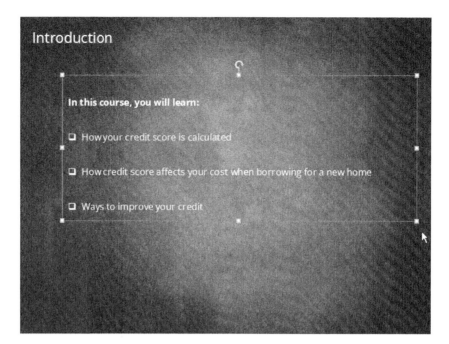

9. Save and close the project.

Images

Storyline lets you import several graphic formats onto a slide including, but not limited to, **BMP** (Windows Bitmaps), **GIF** (Graphics Interchange Format), **JPG** or **JPEG** (Joint Photographic Expert Group), and **PNG** (Portable Network Graphics).

Student Activity: Add an Image to a Slide

1. Open the **ImageMe** project from the Storyline360Data folder.

2. Insert an image onto the main master slide.

   ☐ select the **View** tab on the Ribbon

   ☐ from the **Views** group, click **Slide Master**

   ☐ select the **first slide** (this is the Main Master Slide)

   ☐ select the **Insert** tab on the Ribbon and, from the **Media** group, click **Picture** (there's no need to click the Picture drop-down menu, just click the middle of the Picture tool)

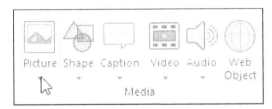

   ☐ from the Storyline360Data folder, **images_animation** folder, open **creditScore-logo**

   By default, images added to slides are placed in the middle of the slide at their original size.

3. Resize the image proportionally.

   ☐ position your mouse pointer on any one of the image's corners

   ☐ drag the resizing handle to make the image approximately one-third its original size

4. Set the Size and Position of the resized image.

☐ right-click the logo and choose **Size and Position**

The Size and Position dialog box opens.

☐ from the left side of the dialog box, select **Size**

☐ from the **Size and rotate** area, change the Height to **70**

☐ change the **Width** to **189**

☐ from the left side of the dialog box, select **Position**

☐ from the **Position on slide** area, change the Horizontal to **0**

☐ change the Vertical to **465**

5. Add Alternative Text.

☐ from the left side of the dialog box, select **Alt Text**

☐ in the **Alternative text** field, type **Credit Score e-Coach Logo**

If your learner is visually impaired, the Alternative text you just added will be read aloud by a screen reader (such as JAWS or HAL). It is a best practice to always add Alternative text to images and is required if you are creating accessible eLearning.

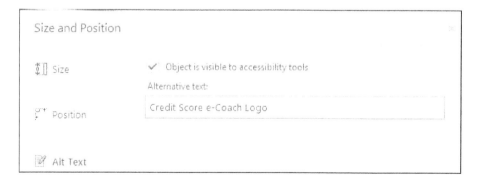

☐ click the **Close** button

6. Change the logo's transparency.

   ❏ right-click the logo and choose **Format Picture**

   The Format Picture dialog box opens.

   ❏ ensure you are on the **Picture** category and then drag the **Transparency** slider right to **60%**

   ❏ click the **Close** button

   By raising the Transparency to 60%, you've made the logo more see-through.

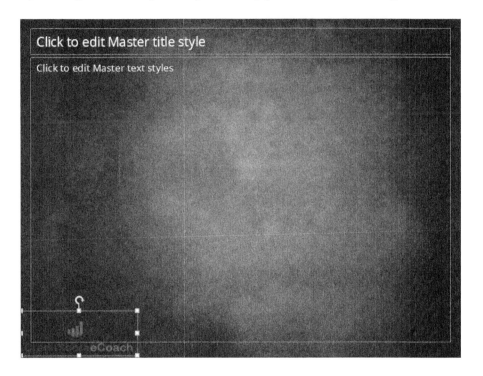

7. Leave the slide master.

   ❏ select the **View** tab on the Ribbon and click **Story View**

   ❏ open slide **1.2 Welcome** (from the **Introduction** scene)

   Notice that the logo has been added to the slide. In fact, the logo has been added to every slide in the project (because you added the logo to the Main master slide which is being used project-wide).

Images Confidence Check

1. Still working on slide **1.2** of the **ImageMe** project, insert the **mycreditscore** image onto the slide (the image is located in the **images_animation** folder).

2. Change the Transparency of the image to **70%**.

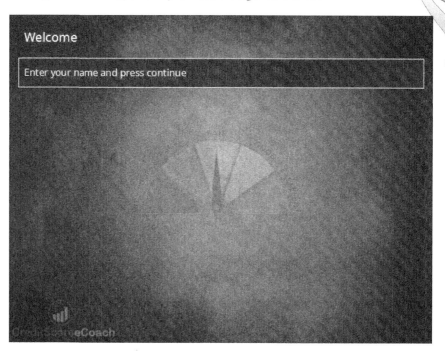

3. Save your work and close the project.

Shapes

If you have used Microsoft PowerPoint, you are likely familiar with Shapes. Similar to PowerPoint, Storyline allows you to insert dozens of different shapes onto a slide. The Shapes can be edited and can contain text.

Student Activity: Add a Shape to a Slide

1. Open the **ShapeMe** project from the Storyline360Data folder.

2. Change the Title for a slide.

   ❑ open slide **2.3 Credit Score Estimator** (from the Credit eCoach scene)

   ❑ on the slide, change the title text **Credit Score Estimator** to **Credit Score Ladder**

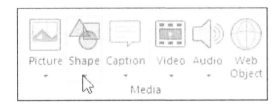

3. Add rectangle shapes.

   ❑ select the **Insert** tab on the Ribbon

   ❑ from the **Media** group, click **Shape**

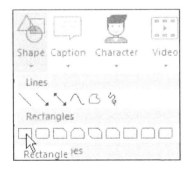

   ❑ from the **Rectangles** group, select the **first shape**

   ❑ on the slide, draw a rectangle anywhere on the slide

4. Change the size and position of the rectangle shape.

❏ right-click the rectangle you just drew and choose **Size and Position**

The Size and Position dialog box opens.

❏ from the **left side** of the dialog box, select **Size**

❏ from the **Size and rotate** area, change the Height to **50** and the Width to **200**

❏ from the left side of the dialog box, select **Position**

❏ from the **Position on slide** area, change the Horizontal to **520** and the Vertical to **300** (**From: Top Left Corner** should remain selected for both options)

❏ click the **Close** button

5. Add text to the rectangle.

❏ ensure the rectangle is still selected and type **High Debt to Credit Ratio**

Shapes Confidence Check

1. Still working in the Credit Score Ladder slide, change the height of the rectangle to **48** and its width to **224**.

2. Duplicate the rectangle and position it just below the first one. (Selecting the edge of the rectangle and pressing [**ctrl**] [**d**] works great for duplicating.)

3. Change the text to **Consolidate Debt**.

4. Duplicate the second rectangle and position the duplicate just below the second one.

5. Change the text in the third rectangle to **Pay On Time**.

6. Duplicate the third rectangle and position the duplicate just below the third one.

7. Change the text in the fourth rectangle to **Close Zero Balance Cards**.

8. Position all four shapes in the lower right of the slide as shown in the image below.

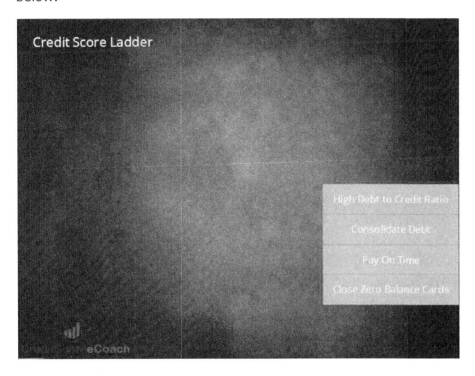

9. Save your work.

Student Activity: Customize a Shape

1. Ensure that the **ShapeMe** project is still open and you are still working on in the **Credit Score Ladder** slide.

2. Draw an L-Shape.

   ❑ select the **Insert** tab on the **Ribbon**

   ❑ from the **Media** group, click **Shape**

   ❑ from the **Basic Shapes** group, select the **L-Shape**

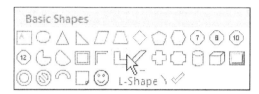

   ❑ draw an L-Shape on the slide (the position and size does not matter yet)

   Notice that there are two yellow resizing anchors on the shape (one at the top, one at the left). The yellow anchors are different than the standard anchors used for resizing. These anchors allow you to reshape the object.

3. Reshape the Shape.

   ❑ drag the yellow anchor at the top of the shape **left** to make the left edge of the L-Shape narrower

   ❑ drag the yellow anchor at the left of the shape **down** to make the bottom edge of the L-Shape shorter

4. Change the Size and Rotation of the Shape.

   ❑ right-click the **colored** part of the L-Shape and choose **Size and Position**

   ❑ with the **Size** category selected, change the Height to **150** and the Width to **120**

   ❑ change the **Rotation** to **90**

Size and rotate			
Height:	150px	Width:	120px
Rotation:	90°		

   ❑ click the **Close** button

Custom Shapes Confidence Check

1. Still working in the Credit Score Ladder slide, duplicate the customized L-Shape four times.

2. Position your shapes so that the end result looks like a ladder similar to the image below. (Note that the bottom left shape is hanging off of the bottom of the slide.)

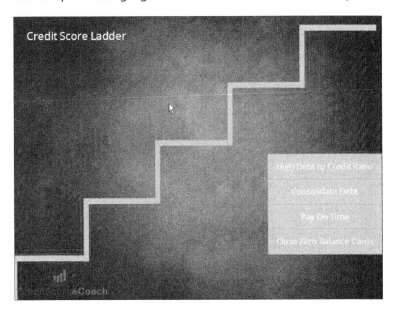

3. Save your work and close the project.

Characters

Storyline ships with several characters that you can use, royalty free, as guides in your eLearning project. You can choose from Illustrated or Photographic characters. Each group contains multiple characters, poses, and expressions. Once added to a slide, Characters can be formatted like any shape or image.

Student Activity: Insert a Character

1. Open the **CharacterCaptionMe** project from the Storyline360Data folder.

2. Insert a Character.

   ❑ open slide **2.3 Credit Score Ladder**

   This is the slide containing the ladder and rectangle shapes you worked with during the last series of activities.

   ❑ select the **Insert** tab on the Ribbon

   ❑ from the **Content Library** group (Storyline 360) or **Media** group (Storyline 3), click **Character(s)**

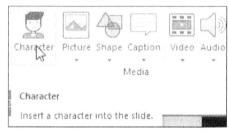

The **Content Library** group in Storyline 360 is shown above; at right, the Storyline 3 **Media** group.

The Characters dialog box opens.

   ❑ if you are using Storyline 360, click **Illustrated Classic** from the list at the left; if you are using Storyline 3, click **Character** from the top

   ❑ select **any Character** you like and click the **Insert** button

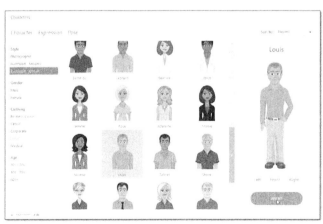

The Characters dialog box looks very different between Storyline 360 (shown at the left) and Storyline 3 (shown above). In addition, if you are using 360, the choices you see may be different than what is shown at the left thanks to updates. In that case, choose **any image** from **any Style** group.

Characters Confidence Check

1. Still working on slide **2.3 Credit Score Ladder**, resize and position the Character as shown in the image below.

2. Ensure that the Character is still selected.

3. From the **Character Tools Design** tab, **Styles** group, click **Character** and select any other Character that you like.

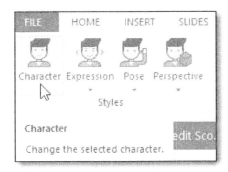

   Notice that although the Character changed, its size and slide position did not.

4. Ensure that the Character is still selected.

5. From the **Character Tools Design** tab, **Styles** group, click **Pose** and select any Pose you like.

6. Insert a new **Title Only** slide beneath slide **2.3 Credit Score Ladder** and title it **Credit Score Resources**. (You learned how to insert slides on page 40.)

7. Display the Characters dialog box and, from the **Photographic** category, select **Atsumi** (but don't close the dialog box yet).

8. With the Characters dialog box still open, click **Pose**.

9. Select and insert the pose shown below.

10. Resize and position the Character so that your slide looks similar to the image below

11. Save your work.

Captions

Captions are similar to Shapes, but they contain pointers that indicate speech or thoughts. You can add text to Captions and format them like any other Shape.

Student Activity: Insert a Caption

1. Ensure that the **CharacterCaptionMe** project is still open.

2. Insert a Caption.

   ☐ open slide **2.3 Credit Score Ladder**

   ☐ select the **Insert** tab on the **Ribbon**

   ☐ from the **Media** group, click **Caption**

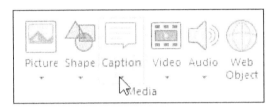

   ☐ select the **Cloud Caption**

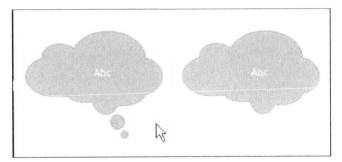

   ☐ draw a caption on the slide just above the Character's head

   ☐ type **I wonder how these factors affect my credit score.**

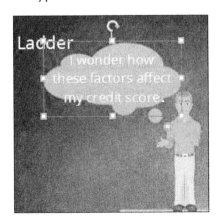

Captions Confidence Check

1. Still working on the Credit Score Ladder slide, resize the caption and format the text as necessary so that your slide is similar to the picture below.

2. Open slide **2.4 Credit Score Resources**.

3. Insert and format a caption similar to the picture below.

4. Save the project.

Content Library

The Content Library is a robust collection of eLearning assets (Templates and Characters) that have been integrated within and work with several of the Articulate tools including Storyline 360.

> **Note:** The remaining activities in this module are only relevant if you are using Storyline 360 (Storyline 3 does not have access to the Content Library). Also, if you are using the trial version of Storyline 360, you may not be able to complete these steps without an active subscription to Articulate 360.

Student Activity: Add a Slide from the Content Library

1. Ensure that the **CharacterCaptionMe** project is still open.

2. Insert a Contact Slide.

   ☐ ensure **2.4 Credit Score Resources** is selected

   ☐ select the **Slides** tab on the **Ribbon**

   ☐ from the **Slide** group, click **Content Library**

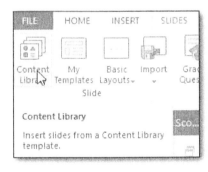

The Content Library dialog box opens containing a library of professionally-designed slides.

   ☐ from the list of categories at the left, select **Closings**

   ☐ from the **Vibrance** group, select **Contact**

❑ click the **Insert Slide** button

The slide is added beneath slide 2.4. It contains placeholder objects that you can replace with your information.

3. Apply a Layout.

❑ on the **Scenes** panel, right-click the new slide and choose **Apply Layout**

❑ choose the **Title Only** layout

Content Library Confidence Check

1. Change the color of the text on slide 2.5 as you see fit.

2. Replace some of the placeholder information at the right with your personal information.

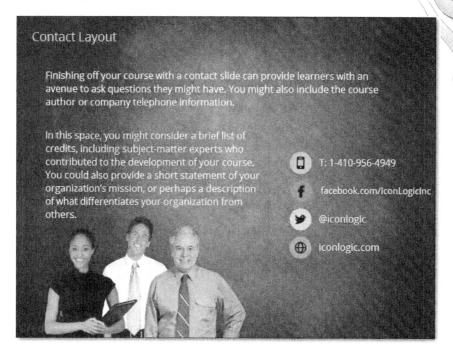

3. Save and close the project.

Module 4: Interactivity

In This Module You Will Learn About:

- Buttons, page 80
- States, page 84
- Layers, page 87
- Text Entry Fields, page 92

And You Will Learn To:

- Add Buttons to Slides, page 80
- Change Button States, page 84
- Create Layers, page 87
- Insert a Text Entry Field, page 92

Buttons

Buttons are the most common form of interactivity that you'll find in just about any eLearning project. Using Triggers (page 96), you can control what happens when the learner successfully clicks a button (such as Go to the next slide or Show Layers).

Student Activity: Add Buttons to Slides

1. Open **ButtonMe** from the Storyline360Data folder and open slide **1.1** (in the Introduction scene).

2. Insert a Continue Button onto the slide.

   ❑ select the **Insert** tab on the Ribbon

   ❑ from the **Interactive Objects** group, click **Button** and select the **second** button in the list

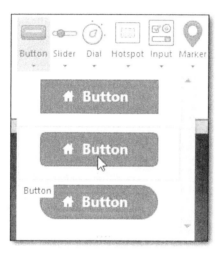

   ❑ draw a button in the lower right of the slide

3. Label and Name a button.

   ❑ with the button selected, type **Continue**

   The text automatically appears within the button and serves as the Label.

   ❑ on the **Timeline**, double-click the name **Button1** and change the **Name** to **Continue Button**

   The **Label** will be seen by your learners when they work through your lesson. The **Name** is never seen by the learner, however it serves as an important development tool for you when working with the Timeline and when you begin working with Triggers.

Newly inserted Buttons do not do anything until you assign a Trigger to them. You'll learn how to work with Triggers later in this module. For now, let's add more buttons to the project.

4. Save your work and close the slide.

   Note: If you are not happy with the appearance of a button, you can always change the way a button looks just like any other shape in Storyline.

5. Open slide **2.2 Factors That Affect Your Credit Score**.

6. Add more buttons to the slide.

   ❑ select the **Insert** tab on the Ribbon

   ❑ from the **Interactive Objects** group, click **Button** and select the **second** button in the list

   ❑ draw a button on the left side of the slide beneath the Subtitle

7. Label and Name another button.

   ❑ with the button you just drew selected, type **Payment History**

   ❑ on the Timeline, double-click the name Button1 and change the name to **Payment History Button**

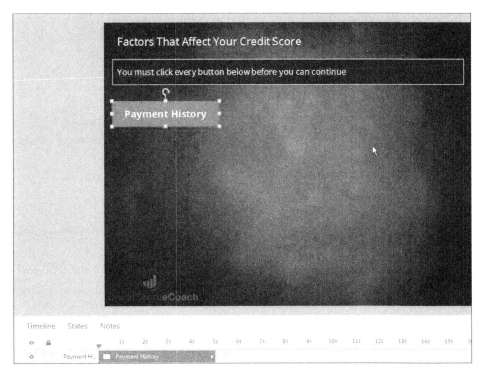

Buttons Confidence Check

1. Still working in the ButtonMe project, duplicate the Payment History button four times. (Pressing [**Ctrl**] [**d**] on your keyboard works great as long as you have the button selected, not the text withing the button.)

   Your slide should now have five buttons.

2. Label the buttons as necessary to match the picture below.

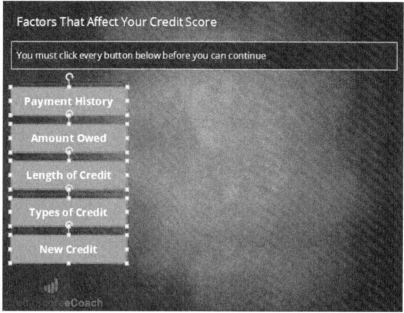

Note: If you want to control the vertical space between selected buttons, Storyline has alignment and distribution controls that are similar to PowerPoint. You can find those controls on the **Format** tab of the Ribbon (within the **Arrange** group).

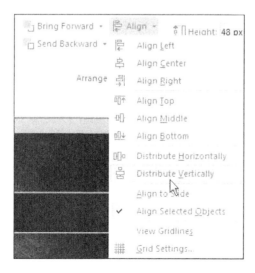

3. Rename the button to reflect the slide Labels.

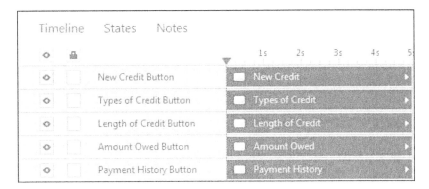

As mentioned above, you can easily change the appearance of selected buttons. If you'd like, spend a few minutes formatting the buttons as you see fit. (You can also elect to leave the buttons as they are because their appearance will have no impact on the remaining activities in this module.)

4. Save your work and close the project.

States

Every button can behave and look differently as the learner interacts with it. For instance, you can assign a Hover State to a button for when the learner hovers above it but does not click it. And you can have the button change color when the learner clicks it. Once the button has been clicked, you can change its appearance yet again (this is known as a Visited State).

Student Activity: Change Button States

1. Open **StateMe** from the Storyline360Data folder.

2. Open slide **2.2 Factors That Affect Your Credit Score**.

3. Edit a button's Visited State.

   ☐ select the **Payment History** button

   ☐ to the right of the **Timeline** tab, click **States**

There are five versions (States) of the Payment History button: Normal, Hover, Down, Visited, and Disabled. The default button State is the Normal State.

   ☐ click the **Edit States** button

   ☐ select the **Visited** Payment History button

Notice that the highlight of a selected State turns from gray to blue.

   ☐ select the **Format** tab on the Ribbon

   ☐ from the **Button Icons** group, select any one of the check marks (you'll need to expand the Button Icons group to see the checkmark icons)

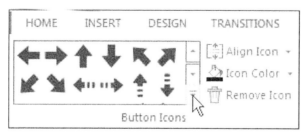

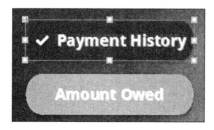

❐ click the **Done Editing States** button

Important! Clicking the **Done Editing States** button is a simple yet crucial step. Should you forget to finish the Editing process and continue editing the slide, those edits become part of the selected State.

4. Save your work.

5. Test the button State.

❐ from the upper right of the Storyline window, click **Preview** and choose **This Slide**

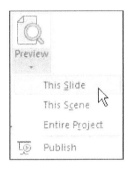

When you Preview a lesson, you're actually getting a sneak peek at what learners experience when they work through your lesson.

❐ click the **Payment History** button

Once clicked, the button turns into its Visited State (you should see a check mark on the button).

6. Close the Preview.

❐ click the **Close Preview** button in the upper left of the Preview window

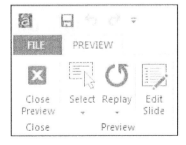

States Confidence Check

1. Still working in the **StateMe** project, edit the **Hover** State of the Payment History button. (Change the color of the button's text to **Blue**.)

2. Click the **Done Editing States** button.

3. Preview the slide.

   This time, the button's text should change when you hover above the button, and a check mark should appear when you click the button.

4. Close the Preview window.

5. Edit the Hover and Click States for the **Amount Owed** button. (Add a check mark for the Visited State and change the text color for the Hover State.)

6. Preview the slide and test the States for both buttons.

7. Close the Preview window.

8. Save and close the project.

Layers

Layers are areas within Storyline that contain just about any slide object. Because Layers have their own Timeline, they behave much like Storyline slides. By default, new Layers are hidden from learner view. You can use Triggers (page 96) to control when the hidden Layers appear on a slide. Every new Storyline project contains one Layer, known as the Base Layer. Every object you have added to any of your slides up to this point have all been added to the Base layer.

Student Activity: Create Layers

1. Open **Finished_CreditScore_eCoach.story** from the Storyline360Data folder.

2. Open slide **2.2 Factors That Affect Your Credit Score**.

3. Preview the slide and click the slide buttons.

   As you click each of the buttons, notice that previously hidden layers containing text appears onscreen. The text you see has been added to Layers, and each button is triggering the appearance of an individual layer. During this activity you'll learn how to add the layers. In the next module, you'll learn how to make the layers appear after the buttons are clicked.

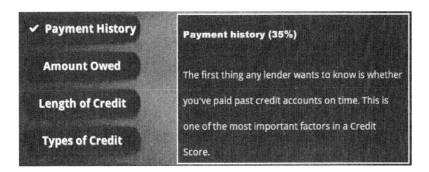

4. Close the preview and **close the project**.

5. Open **LayerMe** from the Storyline360Data folder.

6. Open slide **2.2 Factors That Affect Your Credit Score**.

   Notice that there is a **Slide Layers** panel at the bottom right of the Storyline window. As mentioned above, every Storyline project contains a single layer by default called **Base Layer**. All slide objects are automatically added to the Base Layer.

7. Create a New Layer.

❑ from the **bottom** of the **Slide Layers** panel, click **New Layer**

The New layer, Untitled Layer 1, is created, selected, and opens. Notice that all of the objects on the Base Layer turn gray meaning that they are cannot be edited.

8. Name the new layer.

❑ on the **Slide Layers** panel, double click the name **Untitled Layer 1** and change it to **Payment History Layer**

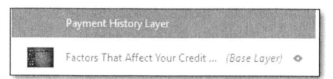

9. Copy content to be used in the Payment History Layer from the storyboard file.

❑ minimize Storyline and open the **Credit-Score-Coach-Storyboards** document with **Microsoft Word**

❑ scroll down to the **Slide: 2.2** section

❑ from the **Programming Notes** section, select and **copy** the text **Payment History (35%)** through **...factors in a Credit Score.**

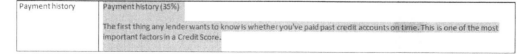

10. Add content to the Payment History Layer.

❑ return to Storyline and the **LayerMe** project (ensure you are still on the Payment History Layer)

❑ paste the text into the **Payment History Layer**

Layers Confidence Check

1. Still working in the **LayerMe** project and slide **2.2**, move and format the text that you pasted onto the **Payment History Layer** as you see fit (just ensure that the text inside of the layer does not cover or obscure the slide's buttons).

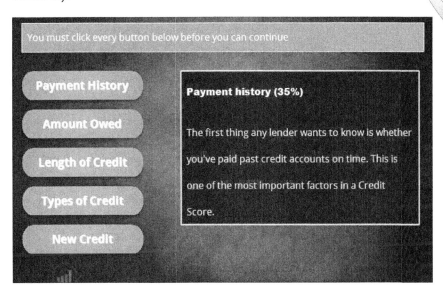

2. Create **four** more layers and rename them as follows:

    Amounts Owed Layer

    Length of Credit Layer

    Types of Credit Layer

    New Credit Layer

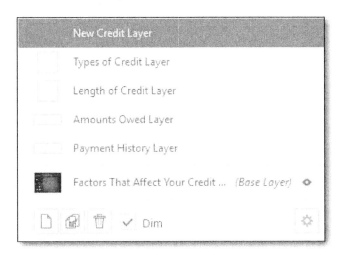

3. From the **Credit-Score-Coach-Storyboards** document, copy and paste the **Amounts owed** text onto the Amounts Owed Layer.

4. Format the **Amounts owed** text similar to the way you formatted the text on the Payment History Layer.

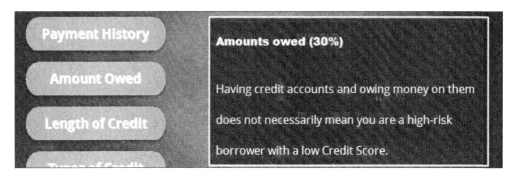

5. From the Credit-Score-Coach-Storyboards file, copy and paste the **Length of Credit** text onto the **Length of Credit** Layer.

6. Format the text similar to the way you formatted the text on the other layers. In addition, add cube bullets to the text as shown below. (You learned how to work with Lists on page 57.)

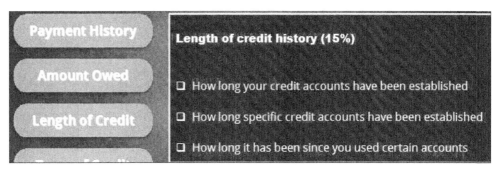

7. From the Credit-Score-Coach-Storyboards file, copy and paste the **Types of Credit in use** text onto the **Types of Credit** Layer.

8. Format the text similar to the way you formatted the text on the other layers.

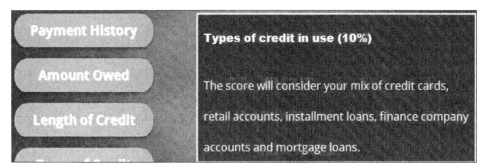

9. From the Credit-Score-Coach-Storyboards file copy, and paste the **New Credit** text onto the **New Credit** Layer.

10. Format the text similar to the way you formatted the text on the other layers.

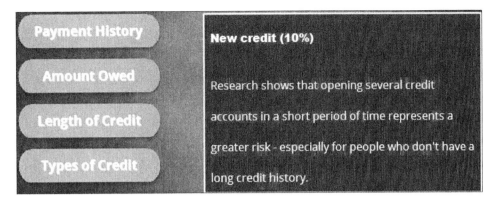

11. Save your work.

As mentioned earlier, you've created several layers, but they're hidden from learner view. In the next module, you'll learn how to use Triggers to make them appear.

12. Close the slide.

13. Close the project.

Text Entry Fields

In a course, can use Text Entry Fields that allow a learner to type data. Learners can be instructed to type specific information into a Text Entry Field and, depending on what they type, captions can provide the appropriate feedback. Once a learner has entered text into a Text Entry Field, the text can be displayed or, by using Variables and Triggers, the data can be reused in several ways.

Student Activity: Insert a Text Entry Field

1. Open **TextEntryMe** from the Storyline360Data folder.

2. Open slide **1.2 Welcome** (the Introduction scene).

3. Insert a Text Entry Field.

   ❑ select the **Insert** tab on the Ribbon

   ❑ from the **Interactive Object** group, click **Input**

   ❑ from the bottom of the Inputs, **Data Entry** group, select **Text Entry Field**

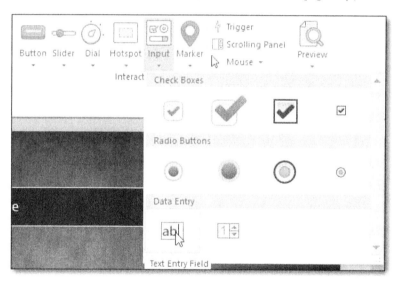

   ❑ draw a Text Entry Field anywhere on the slide

4. Replace the Text Entry Field text and position the object.

   ❑ replace the text in the Text Entry Field with **Enter your name here**

   ❑ position the Text Entry Field similar to the image below

5. Rename the Text Entry Field.

   ❏ at the left of the Timeline, change the name Text Entry to **Learner Name**

6. Preview the slide.

7. Type your name into the Text Entry Field.

   The text you just typed has been stored within a Variable. During the next module, you will learn how to use Variables and Triggers that allow you to reference the text.

8. Close the preview.

Text Entry Field Confidence Check

1. Format the text inside the Text Entry Field as you see fit.

2. Add a button beneath the Text Entry Field with the label **Continue**. (You learned how to insert and format buttons beginning on page 80.)

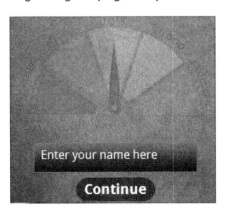

3. Save and close the project.

Notes

iCONLOGiC

"Skills and Drills" Learning

Module 5: Triggers and Hotspots

In This Module You Will Learn About:

And You Will Learn To:

Triggers

Triggers are the key to managing interactivity in your Storyline eLearning courses. Triggers can be attached to slides or slide objects. They control what happens when a learner interacts with a slide object or enters or leaves a slide. For instance, in the Credit Score eCoach you have been building since the beginning of this book, there are multiple buttons on slide **2.2** of the **Your Credit Score** scene. During this module you will add Triggers to each of the buttons that will cause hidden Layers to appear or disappear. You'll also add a Continue button that moves the learner to a different slide, and you'll create a Trigger that adds a lightbox.

Student Activity: Delete Default Triggers

1. Open **TriggerMe** from the Storyline360Data folder.

2. Open slide **1.1 Introduction**.

   The **Triggers** panel (on the right side of the Storyline window) is where you manage all of a project's Triggers. By default, the Triggers panel includes a few **Jump to** Triggers that move learners to the next or previous slides. Because slide 1.1 is the first slide in the scene, you don't need the **Jump to previous slide** Trigger. And the **Continue Button** on the slide takes the place of the player's **Jump to next slide** Trigger. Because the Triggers on the Triggers panel aren't necessary, you'll delete them.

3. Delete Triggers.

   ❑ on the **Triggers** panel, select the first **Jump to next slide** Trigger

   ❑ on the toolbar at the top of the **Triggers** panel, click **Delete the selected trigger**

   ❑ click the **Yes** button to confirm the action

Deleting Triggers Confidence Check

1. Still working in the **TriggerMe** project, delete both Player Triggers from the **Triggers** panel (Jump to next slide and Jump to Previous slide) so that only the Continue Button remains.

2. Save your work.

Student Activity: Add a Trigger to a Button

1. Ensure that the **TriggerMe** project is still open and you're working on slide **1.1 Introduction**.

2. Add a **Jump to slide** Trigger to a button.

   ❒ on the slide, select the **Continue** button

   You can add a Trigger to a button easily via the Triggers panel. The Trigger can result in any number of actions. For instance, a Trigger can move a learner to a different slide, open a web page, show or hide a layer, open a lightbox, or change the state of an object (to name a few).

   ❒ on the **Triggers** panel, click **Create a new trigger**

   The Trigger Wizard opens.

   ❒ from the **Action** drop-down menu, ensure **Jump to slide** is selected

   ❒ from the **Slide** drop-down menu, ensure **next slide** is selected

   ❒ from the **When** drop-down menu, ensure **User clicks** is selected

   ❒ from the **Object** drop-down menu, ensure **Continue button** is selected

   Note: While you were asked to select the Continue on the slide prior to creating the Trigger, pre-selecting an object is not necessary since you can select any slide object from the Object drop-down menu.

   ❒ click the **OK** button

---

3. Preview the scene and test the Trigger.

   ❒ click **Preview** and choose **This Scene**

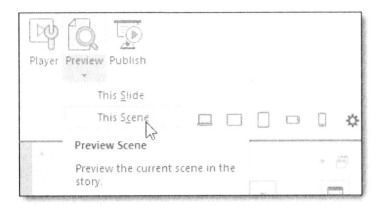

   ❒ on the Preview, click the **Continue** button to jump to the next slide

   ❒ on the **Welcome** slide, click the **Prev** button to move back to the Introduction slide

   ❒ on the **Introduction** slide, click the **Next** button in the lower right of the slide

Because you deleted the Player Triggers during the last activity, the **Prev** and **Next** buttons on this slide don't do anything. (They're not necessary because the Continue button you added is controlling the action.) In this instance, it's a good idea to hide the unneeded player buttons from the slide.

   ❒ close the Preview

Student Activity: Hide Player Buttons

1. Ensure that the **TriggerMe** project is still open and you're working on slide **1.1 Introduction**.

2. Hide Player Buttons.

   ☐ on the bottom of the **Slide Layers** panel, click **Properties** (the Gear icon shown below)

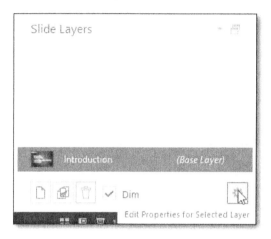

   The **Slide Properties** dialog box opens.

   ☐ from the **Slide navigation and gestures** area, deselect all **Prev** and **Next** check boxes

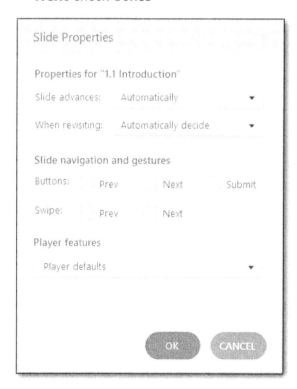

   ☐ click the **OK** button

3. Preview the scene.

4. On the Preview, notice that the Player buttons have been removed from slide **1.1** and the only way to navigate is by clicking the **Continue** button.

5. Close the Preview.

Adding Triggers Confidence Check

1. Still working in the **TriggerMe** project, remove the Player Next button from slide **1.2**.

2. On slide **1.2**, add a Trigger to the **Continue** button that Jumps to the next slide.

   Note: The last step gave you an opportunity to add another trigger to a slide object. Because there are no other slides in the scene, if you were to preview the project and test the button action it would not take you anywhere. You'll be editing trigger actions later in this module that will jump you to a slide in a different scene. For now, you can leave the errant action alone.

3. Save your work.

4. Close any open slides and return to Story View.

Student Activity: Add Triggers to Layers

1. Ensure the **TriggerMe** project is still open.

2. Open slide **2.2 Factors That Affect Your Credit Score**.

3. Add a Trigger to a button that displays a hidden layer.

   ❏ on slide 2.2, click the **Payment History** button

   ❏ on the **Triggers** panel, click **Create a new trigger**

   The Trigger Wizard opens.

   ❏ from the **Action** drop-down menu, choose **Show layer**

   ❏ from the **Layer** drop-down menu, choose **Payment History Layer**

   ❏ from the **When** drop-down menu, ensure **User clicks** is selected

   ❏ from the **Object** drop-down menu, ensure **Payment History Button** is selected

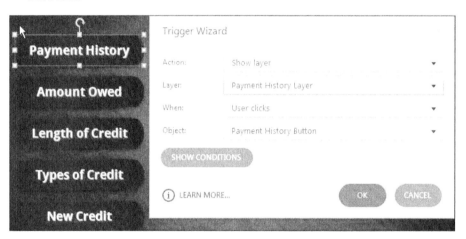

   ❏ click the **OK** button

4. Preview the slide and click the **Payment History** button.

   The Payment History Layer should appear when the Payment History button is clicked.

5. Close the Preview.

Showing Layers Confidence Check

1. Still working in the **TriggerMe** project, slide **2.2**, add Triggers to the remaining buttons that display their corresponding layers.

2. Preview the slide and test the Triggers.

   Notice that when you click from button to button, the previous layer automatically hides, which is awesome. When you're done clicking the final button, it would be nice if the last layer hides as well. You'll take care of that next by adding a Hide Layer trigger to each layer.

3. Close the Preview.

4. Save your work and close the project.

Student Activity: Add a Hide Layer Trigger

1. Open **HideLayerMe** from the Storyline360Data folder.

2. Add a Hide layer trigger to a layer object.

    ❏ open slide **2.2**

    ❏ on the **Slide Layers** panel, select the **Payment History Layer**

    Notice that a simple object (the circle with an X) has been added to the layer (and all of the other layers as well). This object was drawn using an oval shape. (You learned how to draw shapes on page 67.) You'll be adding a Trigger to this shape that hides the open layer.

    ❏ select the shape (the circle with the X)

    ❏ on the **Triggers** panel, click **Create a new trigger**

    The Trigger Wizard opens.

    ❏ from the **Action** drop-down menu, choose **Hide layer**

    ❏ from the **Layer** drop-down menu, ensure **This Layer** is selected

    ❏ from the **When** drop-down menu, ensure **User clicks** is selected

    ❏ from the **Object** drop-down menu, ensure **Oval 1** is selected

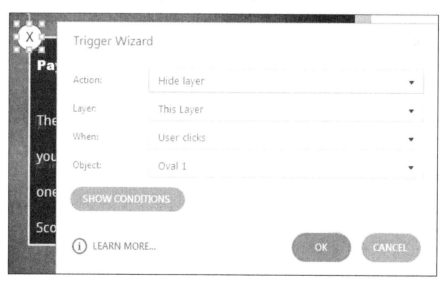

    ❏ click the **OK** button

3. Preview the slide and click the **Payment History** button.

    The hidden **Payment History Layer** should appear.

4. Click the oval object to close the layer.

5. Close the Preview.

Hide Layers Confidence Check

1. Still working in the **HideLayerMe** project, slide **2.2**, add a **Hide layer** trigger to the oval object on the remaining layers.

2. Preview the slide and test the Triggers.

3. Close the Preview.

4. Save your work.

Student Activity: Add a Slide Trigger

1. Ensure that the **HideLayerMe** project is still open and you are working on side 2.2.

2. On the Slide Layers panel, select the **Base Layer**.

3. Add a slide Trigger.

   ❏ ensure that nothing on slide **2.2** is selected and then, on the **Triggers** panel, click **Create a new trigger**

   The Trigger Wizard opens.

   ❏ from the **Action** drop-down menu, choose **Change state of**

   ❏ from the **On Object** drop-down menu, choose **Next Button**

   ❏ from the **To State** drop-down menu, choose **Hidden**

   ❏ from the **When** drop-down menu, ensure that **Timeline starts** is selected

   ❏ from the **Object** drop-down menu, ensure that **2.2 Factors That Affect Your Credit Score** is selected

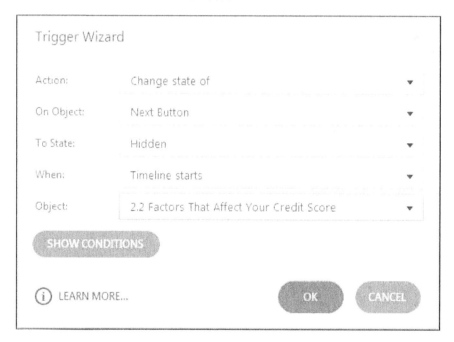

   ❏ click the **OK** button

4. Preview the slide and notice that the **Next** button (typically in the lower right of the slide) is hidden. Learners will not be able to move forward in the lesson until they have interacted with every button on the slide. Next you'll add a conditional Trigger that takes that behavior into account.

5. Close the Preview.

Student Activity: Add a Conditional Trigger

1. Ensure that the **HideLayerMe** project is still open and you are working on side **2.2**.

2. On the Slide Layers panel, ensure that you are working on the **Base Layer**.

3. Add a conditional Trigger.

   ❏ ensure that nothing on slide **2.2** is selected and then, on the **Triggers** panel, click **Create a new trigger**

   The Trigger Wizard opens.

   ❏ from the **Action** drop-down menu, ensure that **Change state of** is selected

   ❏ from the **On Object** drop-down menu, choose **Next Button**

   ❏ from the **To State** drop-down menu, ensure that **Normal** is selected

   ❏ from the **When** drop-down menu, choose **State**

   ❏ from the **On** drop-down menu, ensure that **All of** is selected

   ❏ from the list beneath **All of**, select all of the buttons (put a check in each of the five boxes)

   ❏ ensure that **Are** is selected from the next drop-down menu

   ❏ choose **Visited** from the final drop-down menu

   ❏ click the **OK** button

4. Preview the slide and notice that there isn't a Next button to take you to the next slide.

5. Interact with all of the slide buttons. When you're finished, notice that the **Next** button automatically appears on the slide.

6. Close the Preview.

7. Save your work.

8. Close the slide.

Student Activity: Edit a Trigger

1. Ensure that the **HideLayerMe** project is still open.

2. Open slide **1.2** (in the Introduction scene).

3. Edit the Continue button's Trigger so that the learner jumps to the first slide of a different scene.

   ❏ on slide 1.2, select the **Continue** button

   Earlier in this module you added a trigger to the button that jumped to the next slide. Because there is no slide 1.3, the action does not do anything. You'll edit the trigger next so that the learner is jumped to a slide in a different scene.

   ❏ on the Triggers panel, click **Edit the selected trigger**

   The Trigger Wizard opens.

   ❏ from the **Action** drop-down menu choose **Jump to slide**
   ❏ from the **Slide** drop-down menu, choose **2.1 Calculate Your Possible...**
   ❏ from the **When** drop-down menu, ensure **User clicks** is selected
   ❏ from the **Object** drop-down menu, ensure **Button 1** is selected

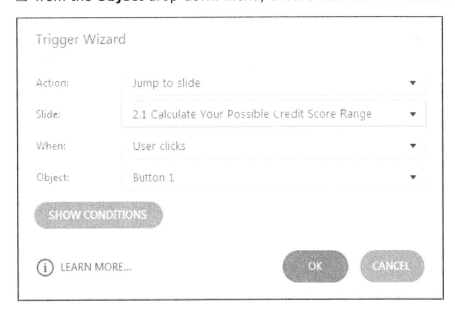

   ❏ click the **OK** button

4. Preview the **Entire Project**.

5. Click the button on slide **1.1** to go to slide **1.2**. Once you're on slide 1.2, clicking Continue takes you to the next scene, slide 2.1.

6. Close the Preview.

7. Save your work.

8. Close the slide.

9. Close the project.

Hotspots

Hotspots are areas of a slide that can be made interactive. You can draw a Hotspot on top of anything that you can see on any slide. Once you've created the Hotspot, you can easily add Triggers to initiate the interactivity.

Student Activity: Add a Hotspot and Lightbox Trigger

1. Open **LightBoxMe** from the Storyline360Data folder.

2. Open slide **4.1 Credit Score Estimator**.

3. Insert an image.

   ❒ select the **Insert** tab on the Ribbon

   ❒ from the **Media** group, click **Picture**

   ❒ from the **Storyline360Data** folder, open the **images_animation** folder

   ❒ open **credit-score-estimator**

4. Resize the image until your slide is similar to the image below.

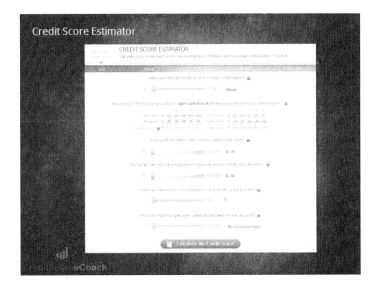

In a moment you'll be adding a Lightbox Trigger to a hotspot. A Lightbox is typically used to display an existing slide in a pop-up window.

5. Close the slide.

6. Open slide **2.4 Credit Score Resources**.

7. Add a Hotspot over a slide object.

   ❒ click the **Insert** tab on the Ribbon and, from the **Interactive Objects** group, click **Hotspot**

❑ select the **Rectangle** hotspot

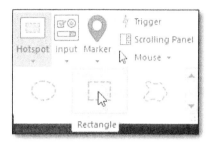

❑ on slide **2.4**, draw a hotspot over the words "Check out this credit estimator resource"

8. Add a Lightbox Trigger to the Hotspot.

❑ ensure that the Hotspot is selected and, on the **Triggers** panel, click **Create a new trigger**

The **Trigger Wizard** opens.

❑ from the **Action** drop-down menu choose **Lightbox slide**

❑ from the **Slide** drop-down menu, choose **4.1 Credit Score Estimator**

❑ from the **When** drop-down menu, ensure **User clicks** is selected

❑ from the **Object** drop-down menu, ensure **Hotspot 1** is selected

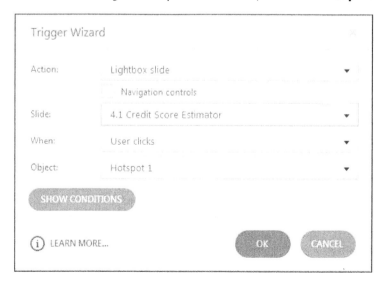

❑ click the **OK** button

Student Activity: Reset the Player Menu

1. Ensure that the **LightBoxMe** project is still open.

2. Reset the player menu.

   ☐ select the **Home** tab on the Ribbon

   ☐ from the **Publish** group, click **Player**

The Player Properties dialog box opens.

☐ select the **Menu** tab

Menu items typically reflect the order of the scenes and slides in the Story View. Currently, the menu and Story View are not the same (slide 2.4 is missing). This disconnect occurs when slides are re-ordered while in Story View (or if someone modifies menu items in the Player Properties). You are going to reset the menu next.

☐ from the bottom of the Menu, click **Reset from story**

☐ click the **Yes** button to confirm the reset.

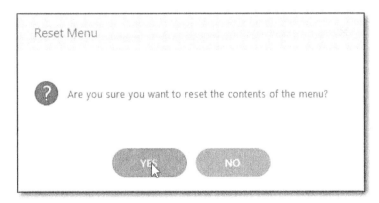

Slide 2.4 has been added to the menu.

☐ click the **OK** button to close the Player Properties

3. Preview the **Entire Project**.

4. Use the Menu at the left to go to the **Credit Score Resources** slide.

5. Click the Hotspot you drew over the text to open the Lightbox slide.

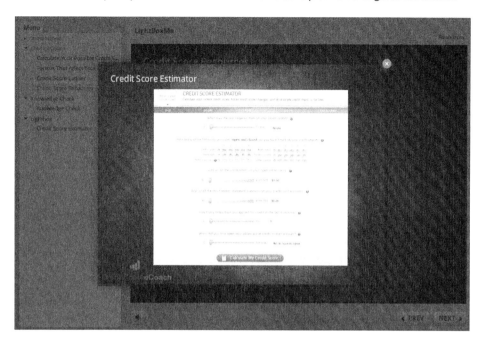

6. Close the Lightbox slide.

7. Close the Preview.

8. Close the slide.

9. Save and close the project.

iCONLOGiC

"Skills and Drills" Learning

Module 6: Variables

In This Module You Will Learn About:

- Variables, page 116

And You Will Learn To:

Variables

Variables serve as buckets for data. The data can be used to provide feedback to the learner and/or allow you as the developer to create conditional scenarios. For instance, you could use a variable to capture a learners name. Once the name has been "stored" by the variable, the name can be displayed over and over again throughout the lesson. In a gaming scenario, variables would allow you to calculate the score for each player.

Student Activity: Manage a Variable

1. Open **VariableMe** from the Storyline360Data folder.

2. Open slide **1.2 Welcome**.

3. Review a default variable.

    ☐ on the slide, select the **Text Entry Field** (you learned how to insert the Text Entry Field on page 118)

    ☐ on the **Triggers** panel, notice that there is already a Trigger assigned to the selected **Learner Name Text Entry Field**

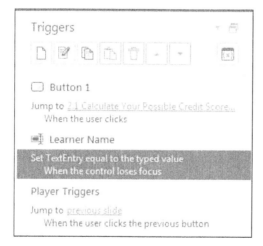

Every time you insert a Text Entry Field in Storyline, the object is assigned a Variable. The variable, as it stands now, is called **TextEntry**. The TextEntry variable stores whatever the learner types into the Text Entry Field once the learner clicks anywhere outside of the Text Entry Field (this is known as an object losing focus).

4. Manage the variable.

    ☐ on the **Triggers** panel, click **Manage project variables**

The **Variables** dialog box opens.

❒ click one time on the current variable name (TextEntry) and rename the variable **learnerName**

Note: Variable names cannot contain spaces or special characters such as exclamation marks and question marks. In the image below, the variable is named with a mixed case naming convention known as **camel casing**. Also, it isn't necessary to select a Text Entry Field prior to managing variables. In fact, you can access the Variables dialog box from any slide in the project.

❒ click the **OK** button

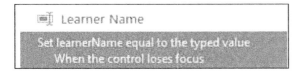

5. Close the slide to return to Story View.

Student Activity: Reference a Variable

1. Ensure that the **VariableMe** project is still open.

2. Open slide **2.1** (in the Credit eCoach scene).

3. Reference a Variable.

   ❏ at the top of the slide, click in front of the word "Calculate" and type **Hello:** followed by [**spacebar**]

   ❏ click the **Insert** tab on the Ribbon

   ❏ from the **Text** group, click **Reference**

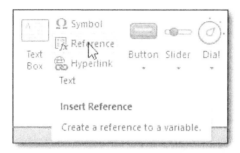

The References dialog box opens. The learnerName variable is available, and because it's the only variable in the project, it's also selected.

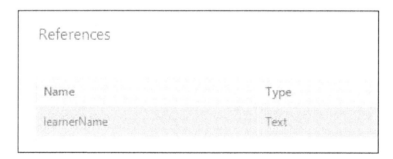

   ❏ click the **OK** button

Storyline inserts a reference to the learnerName variable that is distinguishable by the percent signs. In the future, you can always insert a reference to a variable by typing it yourself (and including the percent signs). Be careful however: if you misspell the variable name in your reference, Storyline has no way to alert you to the error. In case of a typographic error, the data stored by the variable will not appear on the slide because Storyline has no way to alert you to the error.

   ❏ type **,** [**spacebar**] after the variable reference

4. Save your work.

5. Preview the Entire Project.

6. When you get to the **Welcome** screen, type your name into the Text Entry Field and then click the **Continue** button.

And like magic, notice that the text you typed has been dropped into the data bucket and, thanks to the variable reference, has been retrieved.

Hello: Biff, Calculat

7. Close the Preview.

8. Close the project.

Student Activity: Create a Variable

1. Open **CreateGameMe** from the Storyline360Data folder.

2. Open slide **2.5 Credit Score Knowledge Game**.

   This slide contains a table created with simple objects. You learned how to add objects and text to a slide on page 54.

   During the steps that follow, you will use variables to create an interactive game. The learner is required to find five things that can increase a credit score. Each time a correct answer is selected, the learner gets a point up to a maximum of 5. When the learner chooses an incorrect answer, a point is subtracted.

3. Create a Number Variable.

   ☐ on the **Triggers** panel, click **Manage project variables**

   The Variables dialog box opens.

   ☐ from the bottom left of the dialog box, click **Create a new variable**

   The Variable dialog box opens. The game you are creating adds and subtracts numbers, so you need to create a Number variable.

   ☐ in the **Name** field, type **totalScore**
   ☐ from the **Type** drop-down menu, choose **Number**
   ☐ leave the **Value** set to **0**

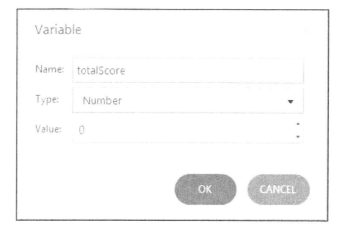

❐ click the **OK** button

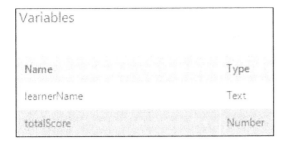

❐ click the **OK** button

Variables Confidence Check

1. Still working on slide **2.5** of the **CreateGameMe** project, insert your new **totalScore** variable into the text box (after "Your score:").

   Need help? See page 118.

2. Preview the slide.

   Because the variable doesn't yet have anything to calculate, you see the default **0** in the text box.

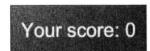

3. Close the Preview.

4. Save your work.

Student Activity: Manipulate a Variable with a Trigger

1. Ensure that the **CreateGameMe** project is still open and you're on slide **2.5**.

2. Create a trigger that will increase the learner score.

   ❏ on the slide, select the **diversify credit types** text box
   ❏ on the **Triggers** panel, click **Create a new trigger**

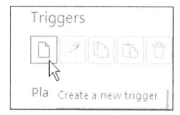

The Trigger Wizard opens.

   ❏ from the **Action** drop-down menu choose **Adjust variable**
   ❏ from the **Variable** drop-down menu, choose **totalScore**
   ❏ from the **Operator** drop-down menu, ensure **+Add** is selected
   ❏ from the **Value** drop-down menu, choose **Value**
   ❏ in the next field, change the value to **1**
   ❏ from the **When** drop-down menu, ensure **User clicks** is selected
   ❏ from the **Object** drop-down menu, ensure **diversify text** is selected

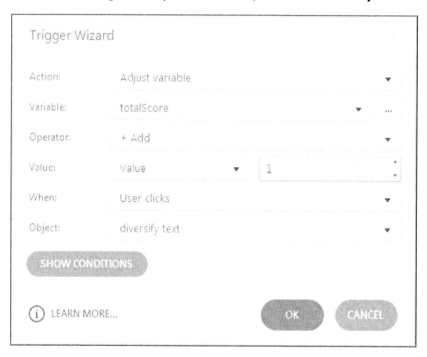

   ❏ click the **OK** button

3. Preview the slide.

4. On the slide, click the **diversify credit types** text.

   Notice that your score increases from **0** to **1**.

5. Close the Preview.

6. Create a trigger that decreases the learner score.

   ☐ on the slide, select the **apply for new credit card** text box

   ☐ on the Triggers panel, click **Create a new trigger**

   The Trigger Wizard opens.

   ☐ from the **Action** drop-down menu ensure **Adjust variable** is selected

   ☐ from the **Variable** drop-down menu, choose **totalScore**

   ☐ from the **Operator** drop-down menu, choose **- Subtract**

   ☐ from the **Value** drop-down menu, choose **Value**

   ☐ in the next field, change the value to **1**

   ☐ from the **When** drop-down menu, ensure **User clicks** is selected

   ☐ from the **Object** drop-down menu, ensure **Apply text** is selected

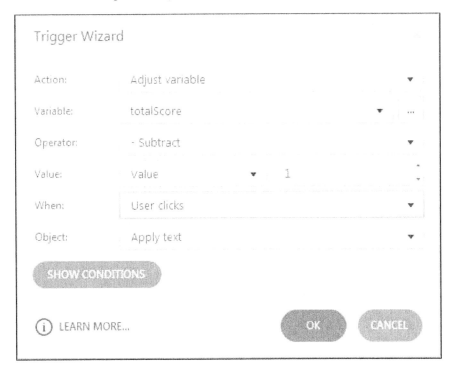

   ☐ click the **OK** button

7. Preview the slide.

8. On the slide, click the **diversify credit types** text.

   Notice that your score again increases from **0** to **1**.

9. On the slide, click the **apply for new credit card** text.

   Notice that your score decreases from **1** to **0**.

10. Close the Preview.

Second Variables Confidence Check

1. Still working on slide **2.5** of the **CreateGameMe** project, create triggers that **increase** the learner's score by **1** for the following text boxes:

   decrease credit to debt ratio

   pay on time

   limit credit score inquiries

   challenge credit score errors

2. Create triggers that **decrease** the learner's score by **1** for the following text boxes:

   close zero balance cards

   borrow from retirement fund

   move debt around

3. Preview the slide.

4. As you click on the slide text, the score increases or decreases by one, as appropriate.

5. Close the Preview.

6. Save and close the project.

Student Activity: Create a True/False Variable

1. Open the **CondtionalTriggerMe** project from the Storyline360Data folder.

2. Open slide **2.5 Credit Score Knowledge Game**.

3. Preview the slide.

   As you click on the slide text, the score increases or decreases by one—this is behavior you tested during the previous Confidence Check. However, you can quickly go past five points or lower than negative four if you click multiple times. During this activity, you will add logic to the game that will ensure that the maximum score is five and the minimum score is negative four.

4. Close the Preview.

5. Add a True/False Variable.

   ❏ on the **Triggers** panel, click **Manage project variables**

   The Variables dialog box opens.

   ❏ from the lower left of the dialog box, click **Create a new variable**

   ❏ name the Variable **apply**

   ❏ from the **Type** drop-down menu, choose **True/False**

   ❏ from the **Value** drop-down menu, ensure **True** is selected

Variable

Name:	apply
Type:	True/False ▼
Value:	True ▼

OK   CANCEL

   ❏ click the **OK** button

True/False Variables Confidence Check

1. Still working in the **CondtionalTriggerMe** project, create the following eight new **True/False** Variables (the Values of each should be set to **True**):

   diversify, decrease, pay, close, limit, borrow, move, and challenge

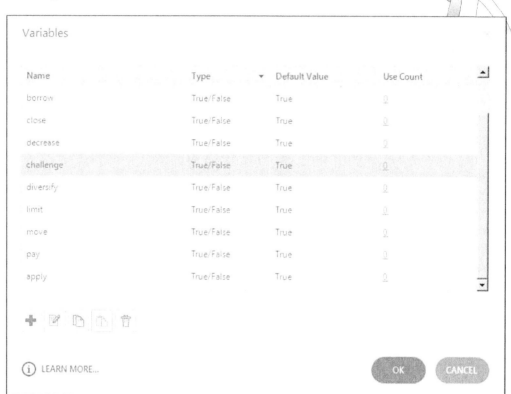

Name	Type	Default Value	Use Count
borrow	True/False	True	0
close	True/False	True	0
decrease	True/False	True	0
challenge	True/False	True	0
diversify	True/False	True	0
limit	True/False	True	0
move	True/False	True	0
pay	True/False	True	0
apply	True/False	True	0

LEARN MORE...

OK   CANCEL

2. Save your work.

Student Activity: Create a Trigger to Change a True/ False Variable

1. Ensure that the **CondtionalTriggerMe** project is still open and you are working on slide **2.5**.

2. Create a Trigger to change a True/False variable.

   ❏ click on the **apply a new credit card** text

   ❏ on the **Triggers** panel, click **Create a new trigger**

   The Trigger Wizard opens.

   ❏ from the **Action** drop-down menu, choose **Adjust variable**

   ❏ from the **Variable** drop-down menu, choose **apply**

   ❏ from the **Operator** drop-down menu, ensure **= Assignment** is selected

   ❏ from the **Value** drop-down menu, choose **Value**

   ❏ in the next field, ensure **False** is selected

   ❏ from the **When** drop-down menu, ensure **User clicks** is selected

   ❏ from the **Object** drop-down menu, ensure **Apply text** is selected

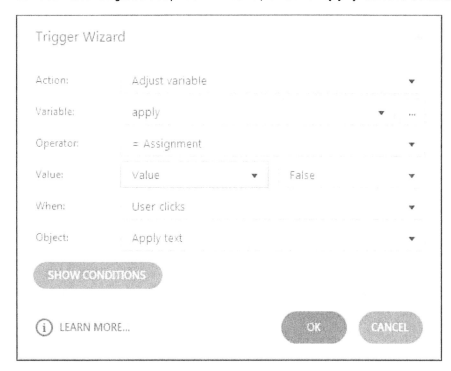

   ❏ click the **OK** button

3. Create another Trigger to change a True/False variable.

   ❏ click on the **diversify credit types** text

   ❏ on the **Triggers** panel, click **Create a new trigger**

   The Trigger Wizard reopens.

❏ from the **Action** drop-down menu ensure **Adjust variable** is selected

❏ from the **Variable** drop-down menu, choose **diversify**

Variable:	diversify

❏ from the **Operator** drop-down menu, ensure **= Assignment** is selected

❏ from the **Value** drop-down menu, choose **Value**

❏ in the next field, ensure **False** is selected

❏ from the **When** drop-down menu, ensure **User clicks** is selected

❏ from the **Object** drop-down menu, ensure **diversify text** is selected

Object:	diversify text

❏ click the **OK** button

Student Activity: Add a Condition to an Existing Trigger

1. Ensure that the **CondtionalTriggerMe** project is still open and you are working on slide **2.5**.

2. Add a Condition to an existing Trigger.

   ❑ on the **Triggers** panel, **diversify text** Trigger, click **Add 1.00 to totalScore**

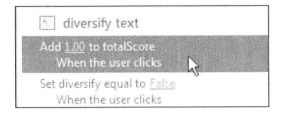

   ❑ from the top of the **Triggers** panel, click **Edit the selected trigger**

   The Trigger Wizard opens.

   ❑ from the bottom left of the dialog box, click the **Show Conditions** button

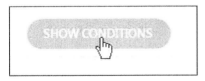

   The **On Condition** area appears.

   ❑ from the lower right of the dialog box, click **Add a new "AND" or "OR" condition**

   The Add Trigger Condition dialog box opens.

❑ from the **If** drop-down menu, choose **diversify**

❑ from the **Operator** drop-down menu, choose **== Equal to**

❑ from the **Type** drop-down menu, ensure **Value** is selected

❑ from the **Value** drop-down menu, choose **True**

❑ click the **OK** button

The Condition you just created has been added to the On Condition area of the **diversify text** Trigger.

❑ click the **OK** button

3. Add a Condition to another existing Trigger.

❑ on the **Triggers** panel, **Apply text** Trigger, click **Subtract 1.00 from totalScore**

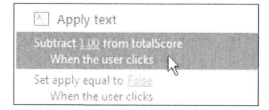

❑ from the top of the **Triggers** panel, click **Edit the selected trigger**

The Trigger Wizard reopens.

❏ from the bottom left of the dialog box, click the **Show Conditions** button

The On Condition area reappears.

❏ from the lower right of the dialog box, click **Add a new "AND" or "OR" condition**

The Add Trigger Condition dialog box reopens.

❏ from the **If** drop-down menu, choose **apply**

❏ from the **Operator** drop-down menu, choose **== Equal to**

❏ from the **Type** drop-down menu, ensure **Value** is selected

❏ from the **Value** drop-down menu, choose **True**

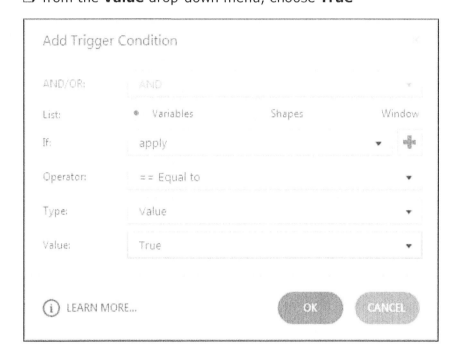

❏ click the **OK** button twice to close both open dialog boxes

4. Save your work.

5. Preview the slide and click the first two answers multiple times.

As you click between the **first two answers**, you'll either lose a point or gain a point... but only one point.

6. Close the Preview.

Conditional Trigger Confidence Check

1. Ensure that you are still working in the **CondtionalTriggerMe** project.

2. For the remaining seven Triggers, create a new Trigger that changes the True/False variables from **True** to **False**. (See page 127.)

3. Add a Condition to each of the **add or subtract** Triggers that limits the addition or subtraction based on the value of the True/False variable. (See page 129.)

4. Preview the slide and click the each of the answers multiple times.

   As you click between the answers, you'll either lose a point or gain a point... but only one point. In fact, if you click every answer, you should end up with one point.

5. Close the Preview.

6. Save and close the project.

Student Activity: Play Audio with a Conditional Trigger

1. Open the **CondtionalAudioMe** project from the Storyline360Data folder.

2. Open slide **2.5 Credit Score Knowledge Game**.

3. Create a Trigger that will play conditional audio.

   ❏ on the **Triggers** panel, click **Create a new trigger**

   The Trigger Wizard opens.

   ❏ from the **Action** drop-down menu choose **Play media**

   ❏ from the **Media** drop-down menu, choose **Audio from file**

   ❏ from the **Storyline360Data** folder, open the **audio** folder

   ❏ open **applause-sound**

   ❏ from the **When** drop-down menu, choose **Variable changes**

   ❏ from the **Variable** drop-down menu, choose **totalScore**

   ❏ click the **Show Conditions** button

   ❏ click **Add a new "AND" or "OR" condition**

   ❏ from the **If** drop-down menu, choose **totalScore**

   ❏ from the **Operator** drop-down menu, choose **== Equal to**

   ❏ from the **Type** drop-down menu, ensure **Value** is selected

   ❏ in the **Value** field, type **5**

☐ click the **OK** button

☐ click the **OK** button

4. Preview the slide and click the each of the correct answers (**diversify**, **decrease**, **pay**, **limit**, and **challenge**).

Once your score reaches **5**, you should be rewarded by hearing an applause sound effect.

5. Close the Preview.

6. Save your work.

Student Activity: Add a Condition to a Button

1. Ensure that the **CondtionalAudioMe** project is still open.

2. Open slide **1.2 Welcome**.

   On this slide, learners are expected to type their name into the text entry field. As it stands now, learners can leave the field empty and still continue with the lesson. You're going to add a condition to the button that requires the learner to type something into the box before being allowed to advance.

3. Add a Condition to the button Trigger.

   ❏ on the **Triggers** panel, select the **Button 1** Trigger

   ❏ on the top of the **Triggers** panel, click **Edit the selected trigger**

   ❏ click the **Show Conditions** button

   ❏ click **Add a new "AND" or "OR" condition**

   ❏ from the **If** drop-down menu, choose **learnerName**

   ❏ from the **Operator** drop-down menu, choose **!= Not equal to**

   ❏ from the **Type** drop-down menu, ensure **Value** is selected

   ❏ ensure the **Value** field remains **empty**

   Leaving the Value field empty is equivalent to **null**, meaning the learner doesn't type anything into the text entry field.

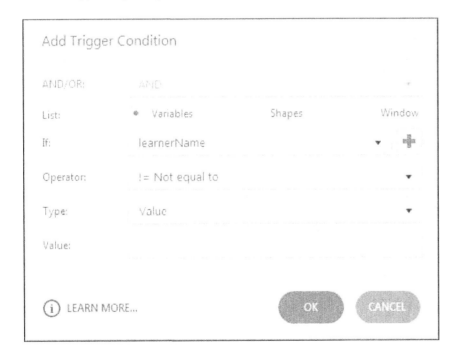

☐ click the **OK** button

☐ click the **OK** button

4. Preview the project.

5. Click the **Continue** button to get to the **Welcome** screen.

6. Try to click the **Continue** button without typing in the Text Entry field.

   Thanks to the condition you added to the button, the lesson should not advance.

7. Close the Preview.

8. Save and close the project.

iCONLOGiC

"Skills and Drills" Learning

Module 7: Audio, Animation, and Video

In This Module You Will Learn About:

And You Will Learn To:

Adding Audio

While you can import several types of audio files into a Storyline project, the most common audio formats are WAV and MP3.

WAV (WAVE): WAV files are one of the original digital audio standards. Although high in quality, WAV files can be very large. In fact, typical WAV audio files can easily take up to *several megabytes of storage per minute* of playing time. If your learner has a slow Internet connection, the download time for large files is unacceptable.

MP3 (MPEG Audio Layer III): Developed in Germany by the Fraunhofer Institute, MP3 files are compressed digital audio files. File sizes in this format are typically 90 percent smaller than WAV files.

You can add audio to slides and, as you learned in the last module, you can use Triggers to control audio. You can also use the Timeline to control when audio plays.

> **Note:** To learn more about digital audio formats, visit
> **www.webopedia.com/DidYouKnow/Computer_Science/2005/**
> **digital_audio_formats.asp**.

Student Activity: Add Voiceover Audio to a Slide

1. Open **AudioMe** from the Storyline360Data folder.

2. Open slide **1.1 Introduction**.

3. Insert audio onto the slide.

   ☐ select the **Insert** tab on the Ribbon

   ☐ from the **Media** group, click the **Audio** drop-down menu and choose **Audio from File**

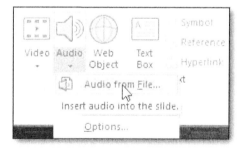

The Insert Audio dialog box opens.

   ☐ open the **Storyline360Data** folder

   ☐ open the **audio** folder and then open **WelcomeToCreditScoreCoach**

The audio is attached to the slide. There are two ways you can tell when audio has been attached at the slide: (1) Just to lower left of the slide, you can see a speaker icon, (2) and the Timeline has an Audio 1 object.

Attaching Audio Confidence Check

1. Preview the slide and, assuming your computer has speakers, listen to the voiceover audio.

2. Close the Preview.

3. Attach the **QuizAudio** voiceover audio to slide **3.1**.

4. Preview slide **3.1** and ensure that you can hear the voiceover talent introducing the upcoming quiz.

5. Close the Preview.

6. Save the project.

Student Activity: Change Slide Audio

1. Ensure that the **AudioMe** project is still open.

2. Replace slide audio.

   ❑ open slide **1.1**

   ❑ on the **Timeline**, select the **Audio 1** object

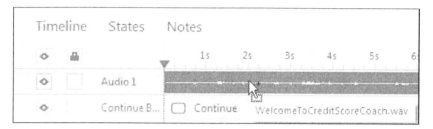

   ❑ select the **Audio Tools Options** tab on the Ribbon

   ❑ click **Change Audio**

   ❑ from the **Storyline360Data** folder, open the **audio** folder

   ❑ open **AudioEditMe**

3. Preview the slide.

   Notice that the audio has some unfortunate gaffes by the narrator. In an ideal world, you would have the voiceover talent provide perfect audio files. However, this audio clip isn't perfect and because you cannot have the voiceover talent re-record, you'll need to edit the audio file directly in Storyline.

4. Close the Preview.

5. Save and close the project.

Student Activity: Edit Slide Audio

1. Open **EditAudioMe** from the Storyline360Data folder.

2. Edit slide audio.

   ❑ open slide **1.1**

   ❑ on the **Timeline**, select the **Audio** object

   ❑ select the **Audio Tools Options** tab on the Ribbon

   ❑ click **Audio Editor**

The Audio Editor dialog box opens.

3. Play the audio.

   ❑ at the bottom left of the dialog box, click the green **Play** button

   A tall blue bar moves across the waveform. This blue bar is known as the Playhead. As the Playhead moves across the waveform, you can see where the gaffes are located.

4. Select and delete part of the waveform.

   ❐ select approximately the first **2.70** seconds of the waveform

   Note: You can tell how much of the audio is selected via the **Select Duration area** of the dialog box (shown in the rectangle in the image below).

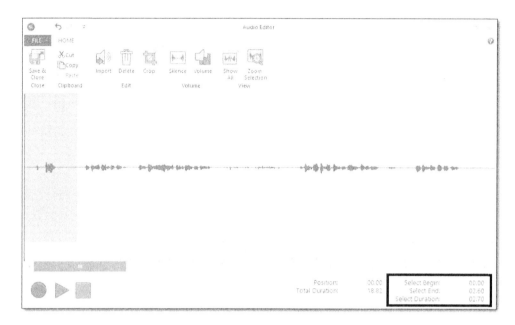

   ❐ from the **Home** tab, **Edit** group, click **Delete**

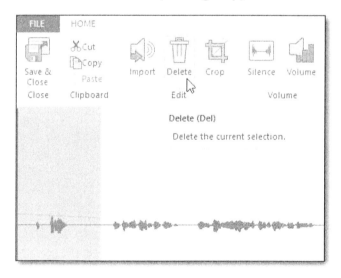

5. Play the audio.

   Notice that the first part of the audio has been deleted.

Edit Audio Confidence Check

1. Still working in the **EditAudioMe** project, delete the remaining gaffes from the waveform.

2. When you are finished editing the audio file, click **Save & Close**.

3. Save the project.

Student Activity: Add Silence

1. Ensure that the **EditAudioMe** project is still open.

2. Add silence to an audio file.

   ☐ still working on slide **1.1**, select the **Audio** object on the Timeline
   ☐ select the **Options** tab on the Ribbon
   ☐ click **Audio Editor**
   ☐ ensure that the Playhead is at the beginning of the waveform
   ☐ at the top of the dialog box, click **Silence**

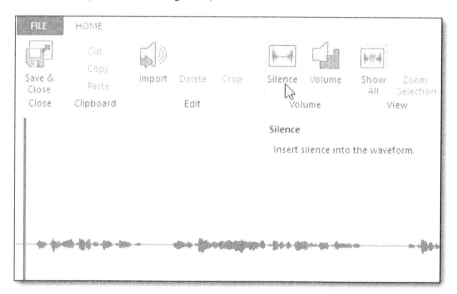

The Insert Silence dialog box opens.

   ☐ ensure that the **Duration of silence to insert** is **1s**

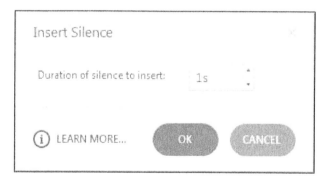

   ☐ click the **OK** button

Notice that a full second of silence has been added to the beginning of the waveform.

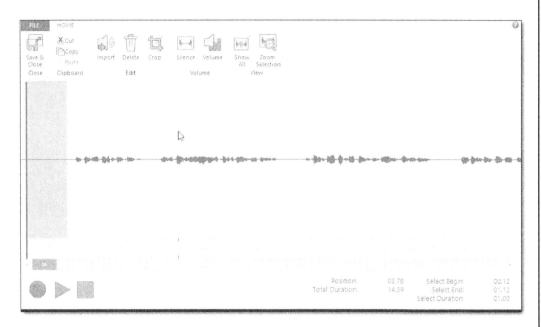

☐ click **Save & Close**

3. Preview the slide and notice how adding one second of silence delays the narration as the slide appears.

4. Save and close the project.

Recording Audio

As you have already learned, you can easily import audio files into Storyline. However, you can also record your own audio. To record audio, you will need a microphone connected to your computer. Once you've got the microphone, consider the following:

Setup: If you plan to use high-end audio hardware, such as a mixer or preamplifier, plug your microphone into the hardware and then plug the hardware into your computer's "line in" port. Set the volume on your mixer or preamplifier to just under zero (this will minimize distortion).

Microphone placement: The microphone should be positioned four to six inches from your mouth to reduce the chance that nearby sounds are recorded. Ideally, you should position the microphone above your nose and pointed down at your mouth. Also, if you position the microphone just to the side of your mouth, you can soften the sound of the letters **S** and **P**.

Microphone technique: It's a good idea to keep a glass of water close by and, just before recording, take a drink. To eliminate the annoying breathing and lip smack sounds, turn away from the microphone, take a deep breath, exhale, take another deep breath, open your mouth, turn back toward the microphone, and start speaking. Speak slowly. When recording for the first time, many people race through the content. Take your time.

Student Activity: Record Voiceover Audio

1. Open the **AudioRecordMe** project from the Storyline360Data folder.

2. Open slide **1.2** (in the Introduction scene).

3. Add a slide Note.

   ❏ at the bottom of the Storyline window, click **Notes**

   ❏ in the **Notes** panel, type **To begin, type your name and then click the Continue button. Please note that the lesson will not move forward until you type your name.**

Timeline States Notes	
To begin, type your name and then click the Continue button. Please note that the lesson will not move forward until you type your name.	

4. Rehearse recording the voiceover audio.

   ❏ with the **Notes** panel open, say the following out loud (as you rehearse the voiceover recording, pay attention to how fast you're speaking... the goal is to record the audio at a medium-paced, comfortable speed):

   To begin, type your name and then click the Continue button. Please note that the lesson will not move forward until you type your name.

5. Set the audio recording options.

❑ click the **Insert** tab on the Ribbon

❑ from the **Media** group, choose **Audio > Options**

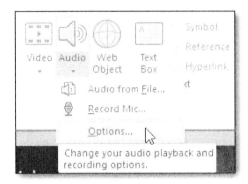

The Audio Options dialog box opens. You can use this dialog box to select a specific microphone for use during the recording process (this is especially helpful if you have more than one microphone attached to your computer). You can also increase or decrease the microphone's volume levels.

❑ from the **Audio Recording** area, select your microphone as necessary (in most cases, the microphone selected by default will work fine)

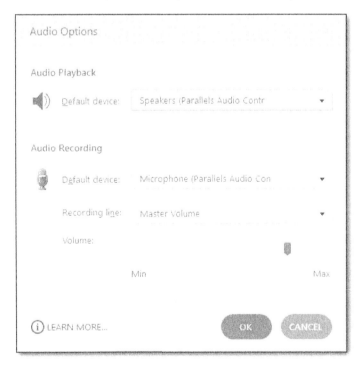

❑ click the **OK** button

6. Open the Record Microphone dialog box.

   ❒ click the **Insert** tab on the Ribbon

   ❒ from the **Media** group, choose **Audio > Record Mic**

The Record Microphone dialog box opens.

7. Display the Narration Script.

   ❒ at the right side of the dialog box, click **Narration Script**

The text you typed (and rehearsed) into the **Notes** area appears in a window. Having the text so close at hand is often helpful during the actual recording process.

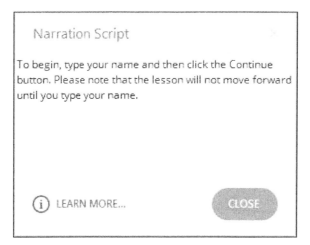

8. Record voiceover audio.

☐ at the far left of the Record Microphone dialog box, click **Record**

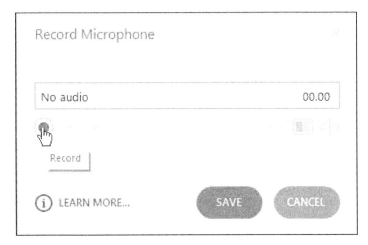

☐ using the Narration Script window, record the following: **To begin, type your name and then click the Continue button. Please note that the lesson will not move forward until you type your name.**

☐ click the **Stop** button

☐ click the **Save** button

9. On the Timeline, notice that an audio object has been added... this is the voiceover you just recorded.

   Note: If you don't have a microphone, you can insert the audio file called **TypeYourName** (from the Storyline360Data, audio folder).

10. Preview the slide to hear the new audio.

11. Close the Preview.

12. Close the slide.

13. Save and close the project.

Adding Animation

You can control the way an object enters a slide via Entrance Animations and control the way an object leaves a slide via Exit Animations. Once you've applied an animation to an object, you can control the timing of the animation and choose from several effects (such as Fades, Swivel, Wheel, and Random bars).

Student Activity: Control Object Timing

1. Open the **AnimateMe** project from the Storyline360Data folder.

2. Open slide **1.1 Introduction**.

3. Preview the slide.

   Notice that the voiceover audio is referring to a list of topics. You want the topics to appear on the screen just as the narrator talks about them. You'll need to delay the appearance of the text by four seconds.

4. Close the Preview.

5. Control an object's Start Time.

   ☐ on the **Timeline** for slide **1.1**, right-click the bulleted list (the object named **Text Box 1**) and choose **Timing**

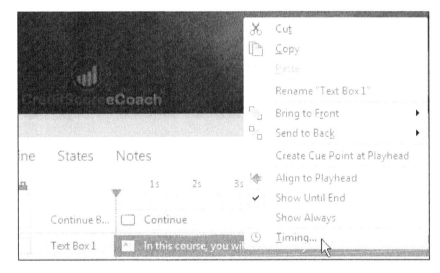

   The Timing dialog box opens.

❏ change the Start Time to **4**

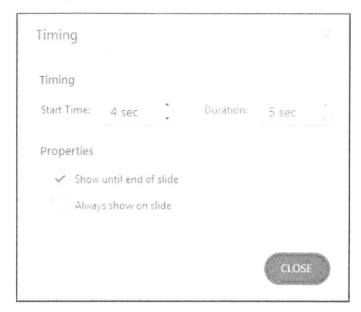

❏ click the **Close** button

On the Timeline, notice that the left edge of the **Text Box 1** object now lines up with the 4-second mark.

6. Show hidden images.

❏ on the Timeline, click **Show/Hide** for each of the four pictures

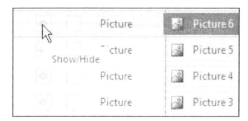

7. Change the Duration for an image.

   ❏ on the Timeline, right-click the first picture (**Picture 3**) and choose **Timing**

   The Timing dialog box opens.

   ❏ ensure that the **Start Time** is **0**
   ❏ deselect **Show until end of slide** (remove the check mark)
   ❏ change the **Duration** to **4 sec**

   ❏ click the **Close** button

Timing Confidence Check

1. Still working in the **AnimateMe** project, change **the Duration** for each of the three remaining pictures to 4 seconds.

2. Save and preview the project.

   Notice that the images appear right away. Then, after 4 seconds, the images disappear and the text appears.

3. Close the Preview.

Student Activity: Animate an Object

1. Ensure that the **AnimateMe** project is still open and that you're working on slide **1.1**.

2. Add an Entrance animation to a picture.

    ❏ on the **Timeline**, select a picture

    ❏ click the **Animations** tab on the Ribbon

    ❏ from the **Entrance Animations** group, click **Animate** and choose **RandomBars**

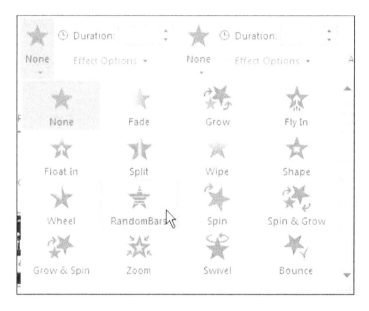

3. Change the animation's Duration.

    ❏ just to the right of **Animate**, change the **Duration** to **00.50**

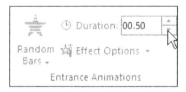

You can tell when an object has an animation attached to it via the animation badge that appears to the left of an affected image.

4. Preview the slide to see the animation.

5. Close the Preview.

6. Add an Exit animation to a picture.

    ❒ on the Timeline, select the same picture (Picture 3)

    ❒ from the **Animations** tab on the Ribbon, **Exit Animations** group, click **Animate** and choose **Fade**

7. Preview the slide and, as the image appears on the slide, notice that the RandomBars animation occurs for one-half second. Then, as the image leaves the slide, the Fade animation occurs.

Animations Confidence Check

1. Still working in the **AnimateMe** project, apply any Entrance and Exit animations you like to a second image.

    Note: Be careful when you select the pictures. If you select a picture on the slide directly, it's easy to accidentally select the text. It's best to select objects via the Timeline.

2. Preview the slide to see your new animations.

3. Hide the slide object named Text Box 1.

4. If you are satisfied with your animations, ensure that a picture with animations is selected and then click the **Animation Painter** (it's just to the left of the Entrance animations).

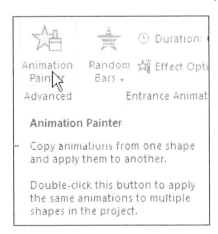

5. Click the other images on the slide to apply (Paint) the same animations to the remaining images on the slide.

6. Show the slide object named Text Box 1 that you hid a moment ago.

7. Preview the slide to see your new animations.

8. Save the project.

Student Activity: Control Animation Options

1. Ensure that the **AnimateMe** project is still open and that you're working on slide **1.1**.

2. Work with Animation Effect Options.

   ❏ on the Timeline, select the bulleted list text (**Text Box 1**)

   ❏ from the **Animations** tab on the Ribbon, **Entrance Animations** group, click **Animate** and choose **Fly In**

   ❏ from just beneath **Duration**, click **Effect Options**

   ❏ ensure **From Bottom** and then, from the **Sequence** area, choose **By Paragraph**

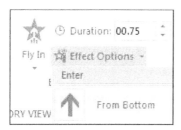

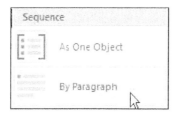

3. Set the Timing for individual paragraphs.

   ❏ at the far left of the Timeline, click the triangle to the left of **Text Box 1** to expand the group

   ❏ on the Timeline, drag the beginning of the second paragraph to **6** seconds

   ❏ on the Timeline, drag the third paragraph to **8** seconds

   ❏ on the Timeline, drag the last paragraph to **11** seconds

4. Preview the slide.

   The text animation should enter from the bottom of the screen and be synchronized with the voiceover audio.

5. Close the Preview.

6. Close the slide.

7. Save and close the project.

Adding Video

You can insert videos into Storyline from just about any video format and video sharing service (such as YouTube and Vimeo). You can also create videos of actions you take on your computer (or your webcam) using Storyline. (You'll learn how to record screen actions beginning on page 183.)

Student Activity: Insert Video

1. Open the **VideoMe** project from the Storyline360Data folder.

2. Open slide **1.2** (the Welcome slide in the Introduction scene).

3. Insert a video onto the slide.

   ❏ click the **Insert** tab on the Ribbon

   ❏ from the **Media** group, click the **Video** drop-down menu and choose **Video From File**

   ❏ from the **Storyline360Data** folder, open the **images_animation** folder

   ❏ open **welcomeToLesson.mp4**

   The video is inserted on the slide. It's pretty large and takes up the entire slide.

4. Preview the slide.

   Notice that the video and the slide audio overlap. The next step will be to adjust the timing of the other slide objects so that they begin to play once the video has finished.

5. Close the Preview.

6. Save your work.

Student Activity: Delay Object Start Times

1. Ensure that the **VideoMe** project is still open and that you're on slide **1.2**.

2. On the Timeline, notice that the **Video1** object plays for **12** seconds. You'll need to set the Start Time of all of the other objects to 12 seconds so that they appear after the video ends. However, doing so will also extend the playtime for the slide and the video. To ensure that the video stops at 12 seconds, you'll deselect the **Show Until End** command.

3. Deselect the Show Until End command.

    ❏ on the **Timeline**, right-click the **Video1** object and deselect **Show Until End**

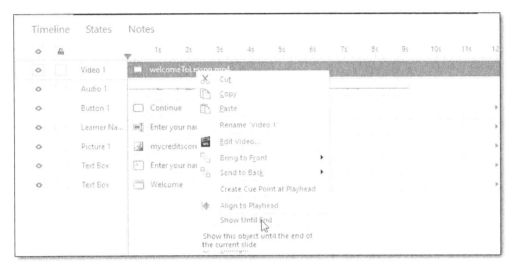

4. Adjust the remaining slide objects so that their Start Time is 12 seconds.

    ❏ on the **Timeline**, select all of the slide objects **except** the video

    Note: You can multi-select Timeline objects by pressing [**ctrl**] and clicking each object in turn, or [**shift**]-clicking contiguous objects).

    ❏ right-click any of the selected objects and choose **Timing**

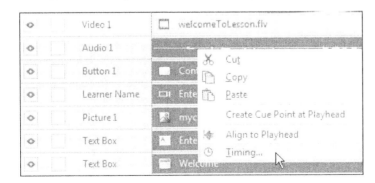

The Timing dialog box opens.

❑ change the Start Time to **12**

❑ click the **Close** button

On the Timeline, notice that most of the slide object now start at 12 seconds.

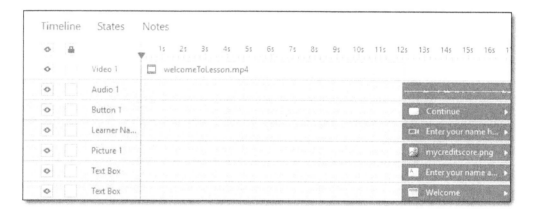

5. Preview the slide.

   Notice that the video plays, disappears, and then the remaining slide objects play. Did you also notice that you can hear the video "director" say "cut" at the end of the video? No worries. You can easily trim that part of the video out.

6. Close the Preview.

7. Save your work.

Student Activity: Trim Video

1. Ensure that the **VideoMe** project is still open and that you're on slide **1.2**.

2. Trim the video.

    ❏ on the **Timeline**, select the **Video1** object

    ❏ click the **Video Tools Options** tab on the Ribbon

    ❏ at the left of the Ribbon, click **Edit Video**

The Articulate Video Editor opens.

    ❏ in the **Edit** group, click **Trim**

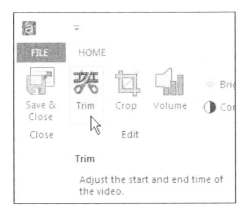

By default, approximately the first and last half-second of the video is selected for Trimming. Trimming the first part a little bit is fine. However, you'll need to extend the trimmed portion at the end a little bit more to totally remove the director's voice.

❏ on the right side of the Video Editor Timeline, extend the **Trim End** to **10:737**

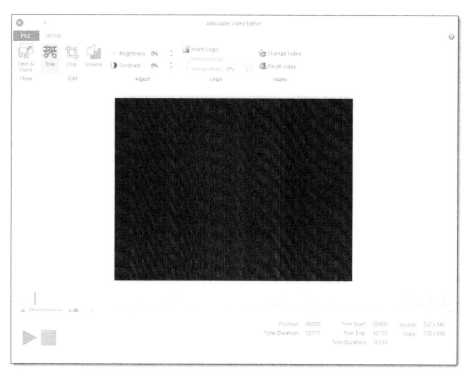

❏ click **Save & Close**

3. Preview the slide.

   Notice that the video has been trimmed just enough to remove the unwanted audio.

4. Close the Preview.

5. Save your work.

Student Activity: Animate a Video

1. Ensure that the **VideoMe** project is still open and that you're on slide **1.2**.

2. Apply an Animation to the video.

   ❏ on the **Timeline**, select the **Video1** object

   ❏ click **Animations** on the Ribbon

   ❏ from the **Exit Animations** group, click **Animate** and choose **Fade**

   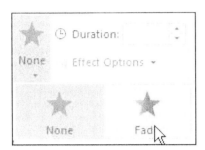

   ❏ change the **Duration** to **1.50**

3. Preview the slide.

   Notice that the animation you added to the video softens the transition between the video and the remaining slide objects.

4. Close the Preview.

5. Close the slide.

6. Save your work and close the project.

Adding Transitions

During the last activity you applied an animation to a video that smoothly moved the learner from one slide object to another. During the following activities you will apply an animation to an entire slide and a slide layer. Applying animations in this manner is known as adding a Transition.

Student Activity: Add a Slide Transition

1. Open the **TransitionMe** project from the Storyline360Data folder.

2. Open slide **2.1**.

3. Apply a Push Transition to the slide.

   ❏ click **Transitions** on the Ribbon

   ❏ from the **Transitions to This Slide** area, click **Push**

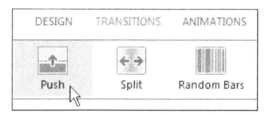

4. Preview the slide.

   Notice that when the slide starts, the Push Transition (from bottom to top) appears.

5. Close the Preview.

Transitions Confidence Check

1. Still working in the **TransitionMe** project, open slide **3.1** and add a Transition.

2. After adding the Transition, locate the **Effect Options** drop-down menu on the Ribbon and experiment with the various menu items.

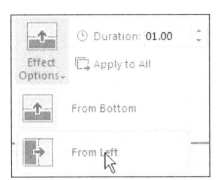

Note: The Effect Options vary based on the transition you choose. Some transitions do not include any Effect Options

3. Preview the slide to see the Transition.

4. Close the Preview.

5. Open slide **2.2**.

6. On the Slide Layers panel, select the **Payment History Layer** and apply a Transition.

7. Preview the slide to click the Payment History button to see the new Transition.

8. Close the Preview.

9. Save and close the project.

Notes

Module 8: Quizzes

In This Module You Will Learn About:

- Quizzing, page 168

And You Will Learn To:

- Insert a Multiple Choice Slide, page 168
- Insert a Matching Drag-and-Drop Slide, page 173
- Insert a Freeform Drag and Drop Quiz Slide, page 175
- Insert a Quiz Result Slide, page 179

Quizzing

Learning can be exhausting. If you think about it, there's only so much learning that can effectively occur over a set amount of time. If you are a trainer, you can elect to force feed information to your students. However, without regularly scheduled breaks, the ability of your students to both learn and retain information is minimized. Beyond giving breaks, you may encourage your learners to openly discuss what they are learning during class. Discussing lessons taught in class greatly improves the students' experience, enhances their understanding of the concepts, and increases their retention of the material.

An eLearning session has no live trainer and no classmates. How is a learner supposed to share the knowledge gained during class when the learner is alone? One solution is to add a quiz. In addition to providing you, as the instructional designer, a way to measure the effectiveness of the course content, the students will be able to think about what they have learned as they answer quiz questions.

Storyline includes a wonderful array of Quiz Slides including Multiple Choice, True/False, Matching, Fill-in-the-blank, Pick One or Many, and even Drag and Drop. During the activities that follow, you'll get a chance to add a quiz and a few questions.

Student Activity: Insert a Multiple Choice Slide

1. Open the **QuizMe** project from the Storyline360Data folder.

2. Open slide **3.1**.

3. Insert a Multiple Choice Quiz Slide.

   ☐ click **Slides** on the Ribbon and, from the **Quizzing** group, click **Graded Question**

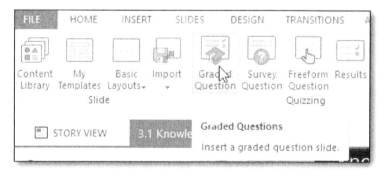

   The Insert Slide dialog box opens.

❏ at the top of the dialog box, select **Multiple Choice**

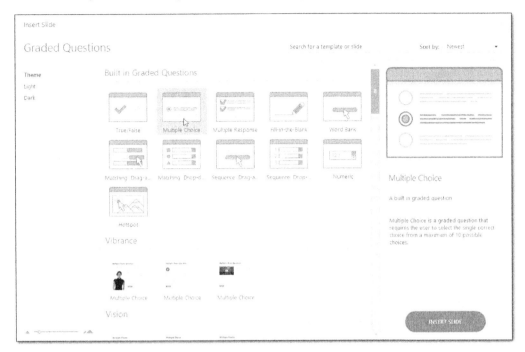

❏ click the **Insert Slide** button

The question opens in **Form View**. You can use this view to add the question text and set up question options such as feedback text and point values.

4. Add the question.

❏ in the **Enter the question** area, type **Which of the following factors contributes 35% to the calculation of a credit score?**

> Enter the question
>
> Which of the following factors contributes 35% to the calculation of a credit score?

5. Add the answers.

❑ to the right of answer **A**, click in the **Choice** area and type **On time payment**

❑ to the right of answer **B**, click in the **Choice** area and type **Debt to credit ratio**

❑ to the right of answer **C**, click in the **Choice** area and type **New credit**

❑ to the right of answer **D**, click in the **Choice** area and type **Type of credit**

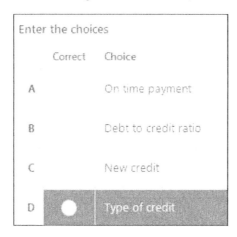

6. Set the correct answer.

❑ to the left of answer **A**, click the radio button

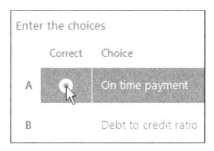

7. Change the point value of the question to 25.

❑ at the bottom of the Form View, notice the **Feedback** area

❑ to the right of the **Correct** Feedback option, click the number **10** in the **Points** area

❑ change the value to **25**

8. Edit the Feedback text.

☐ to the left of the 25, click the **More** button

The resulting **Feedback** dialog box presents you with an opportunity to change the Feedback text, add audio, and control where the learner goes after answering the question correctly (Branch to the following).

☐ at the top of the Feedback dialog box, replace the existing text with **That's right! On time payment is correct.**

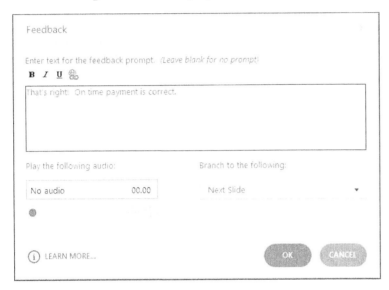

☐ click the **OK** button

On the Ribbon, notice that the options are now question slide specific. For instance, you can add **Audio** to the slide, insert **Media**, change the number of **Attempts**, and more.

9. Switch to Slide View.

☐ from the **Question** panel (at the far right of the Storyline window), click **Slide View**

You can use the Question panel to quickly switch between Slide and Form View, allowing you to edit the question options and text as needed. Notice also

---

that two additional layers have been added in Slide Layers. These new layers contain the feedback text. You can edit the content on the layers as you can with any Storyline layer.

Your question slide should look like this:

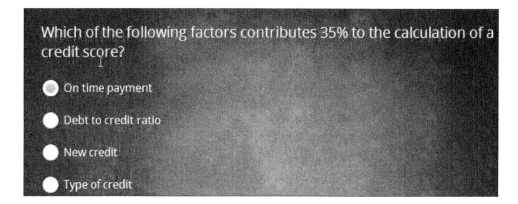

10. Preview the slide and answer the question.

    If you answer the question correctly and click Submit, you'll see the feedback text you edited a moment ago. If you answer incorrectly and click Submit, you'll see the default feedback text.

11. Close the Preview.

12. Save your work.

Student Activity: Insert a Matching Drag-and-Drop Slide

1. Ensure that the QuizMe project is still open.

2. Insert another quiz slide.

   ☐ on the **Scenes** panel, select slide **3.2**

   ☐ click **Slides** on the Ribbon and, from the **Quizzing** group, click **Graded Question**

   The Insert Slide dialog box reopens.

   ☐ select **Matching Drag-and-Drop**

   ☐ click the **Insert Slide** button

   The question opens in Form View.

3. Add the question.

   ☐ in the **Enter the question** area, type **Drag each percentage to its matching credit score factor.**

4. Add the Choices and Matches.

   ❏ for **Choice A**, type **Payment History** in the **Choice** column

   ❏ to the right of Payment History, type **35%** in the **Match** column

   ❏ edit the remaining options to match the picture below

Enter the choices		
	Choice	Match
A	Payment History	35%
B	Amount Owed	30%
C	Length of Credit	15%
D	Type of Credit	10%

5. Switch to Slide View and preview the slide.

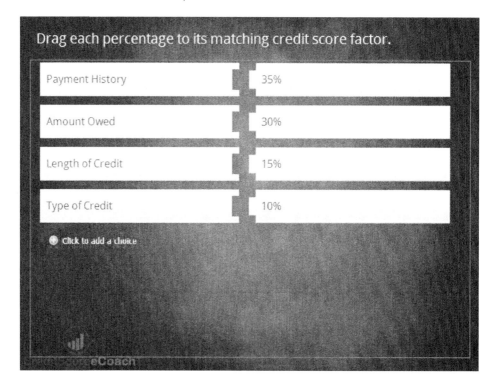

6. Drag the percentage answers to the text at the left and then click the **Submit** button to see if you answered correctly.

7. Close the Preview.

8. Save your work.

Student Activity: Insert a Freeform Drag and Drop Quiz Slide

1. Ensure that the QuizMe project is still open.

2. Insert a Freeform quiz slide.

   ❏ on the **Scenes** panel, select slide **3.3**

   ❏ click **Slides** on the Ribbon and, from the **Quizzing** group, click **Freeform Question**

   The Insert Slide dialog box reopens.

   ❏ select **Drag and Drop**

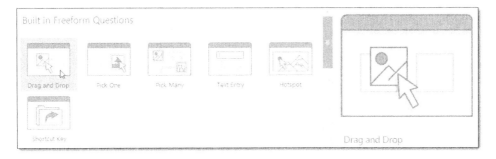

   ❏ click the **Insert Slide** button

   Unlike the last two questions you inserted, after inserting the Drag and Drop slide, you are taken to Slide View instead of Form View. You'll be inserting four images onto the question slide, something you cannot do while in the Form View.

3. Add four images onto the slide.

   ❏ click the **Insert** tab on the **Ribbon**

   ❏ from the **Media** group, click **Picture**

   ❏ from the **Storyline360Data** folder, open **images_animation**

   ❏ select and **open** the following **four** images: **debt-credit-ratio**, **length-of-credit-**, **payment-history**, and **types-of-credit**

   Four clipboard images are inserted in the middle of the slide, and are positioned on top of each other.

❏ move the images around the slide until your slide is similar to the picture below (leave room at the top and the left of the slide for some text that you will add next)

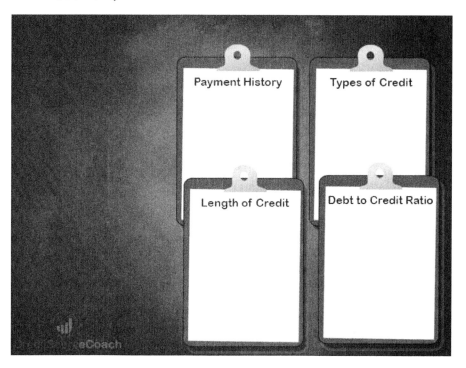

4. Apply a **Title Only** layout to slide 3.4. (You learned about applying a layout on page 46.)

5. Replace the existing title text with **Drag each percentage over its corresponding target.**

6. Insert four text boxes onto the slide with the text 35%, 30%, 15%, and 10%. (You learned about text boxes on page 54.)

7. Format and position each of the four text boxes so that they are similar to the picture below.

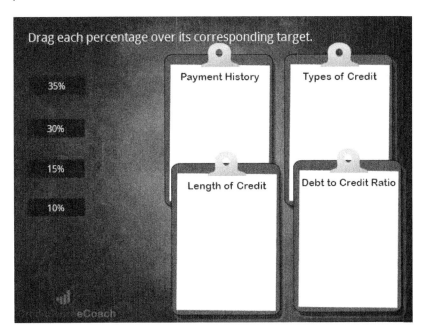

8. On the Timeline, name the new text boxes to match the text within each box. (You learned about naming objects on page 80.)

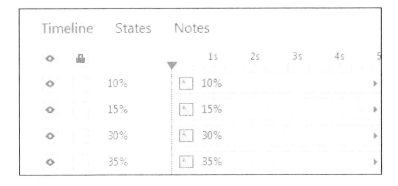

9. Associate the drag items and drop targets.

   ☐ on the **Question** panel, click **Form View**

   ☐ in the **Drag Item** column, click where it says **Click to enter a choice**

   ☐ from the drop-down menu, choose **35%**

   ☐ in the **Drop Target** column, click **(None)** and choose **Picture 3 - payment-history-.png**

Quiz Confidence Check

1. Associate the remaining drag items and drop targets as shown in the picture below.

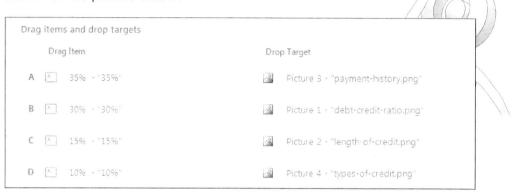

2. Return to slide view and preview the slide. (You should be able to drag each item at the left onto a clipboard and then Submit an answer.)

3. Insert a **True/False** slide beneath slide **3.4** that matches the picture below.

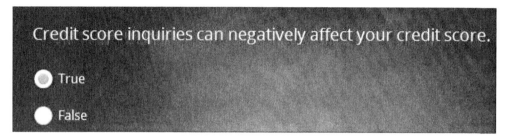

4. Use **Form View** to change the points for the correct answer on slides **3.3**, **3.4**, and **3.5** from **10** to **25**

5. Preview the **scene** and take the quiz.

6. When finished, close the preview.

7. Save your work.

Student Activity: Insert a Quiz Result Slide

1. Ensure that the QuizMe project is still open.

2. Select slide 3.5.

3. Insert a Quiz Result Slide.

   ❑ click **Slides** on the Ribbon and, from the **Quizzing** group, click **Results**

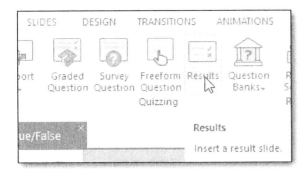

The Insert Slide dialog box reopens.

❑ at the top of the dialog box, select **Grade Results Slide**

❑ click the **Insert Slide** button

The Result Slide Properties dialog box opens. By default, all of the questions you have added to the quiz will be counted in the final score.

❏ at the bottom of the dialog box, change the **Passing Score** to **75**

❏ click the **OK** button

4. Allow users to print the quiz results.

❏ on the Ribbon, click **Result Tools**, **Design**

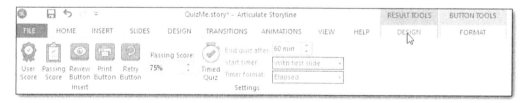

❏ from the **Insert** group, click **Print Button**

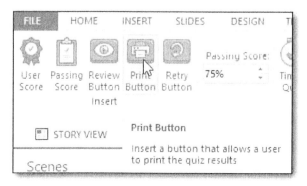

5. On the slide, draw a button similar to the image below.

6. Preview the **scene** and take the quiz. (When finished with the quiz this time, you'll see the results slide.)

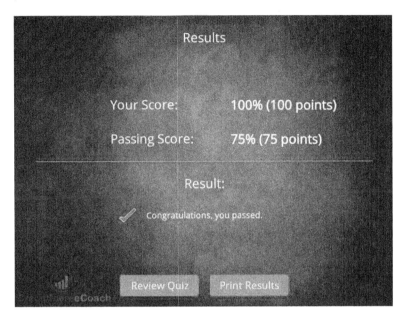

7. Close the Preview.

8. Save your work and close the slide.

9. Close the project.

Notes

iCONLOGiC
"Skills and Drills" Learning

Module 9: Recording and Publishing

In This Module You Will Learn About:

- Recording Screen Actions, page 184
- Player Settings, page 192
- Publishing, page 203

And You Will Learn To:

- Rehearse a Script, page 186
- Record a Video, page 187
- Edit Player Properties, page 192
- Reorder Slides and Edit Triggers, page 197
- Publish Course Content, page 203

Recording Screen Actions

Typical Storyline projects consist of multiple slides, similar to Microsoft PowerPoint. You can create a blank Storyline project and insert slides, just like you learned to do beginning on page 30. If you need pictures of your software application, you can use any one of several programs to create screen captures. For instance, we use SnagIt (**www.snagit.com**) and FullShot (**www.fullshot.com**). In fact, FullShot was used to create all of the screen captures in this book. Any screen captures you create using a screen capture application can easily be inserted onto a Storyline slide (you learned how to insert images on page 63).

Most people who create software simulations and demonstrations use Storyline to create the screen captures. There are four ways to use any recording you create with Storyline: (1) **Video Mode** (a recording of what you're doing on screen that is not interactive), (2) **View Mode** (a step-by-step demonstration of what you did in the computer), (3) **Try Mode** (an interactive, step-by-step version of what you recorded), and (4) **Test Mode** (an interactive, step-by-step version that is scored). The four recording types can be grouped into two categories: video and slide-by-slide. When you insert the Video recording into a project, you'll end up with a slide that contains the entire video. When you use the View, Try, or Test Modes, you'll end up with several slides in the project (one slide for every click you made with your mouse during the recording process). The mode you use in your project depends on your training goal. When you want your learner to interact with recording, insert the Try or Test versions. When you want to demonstrate a concept (and aren't concerned about interactivity), insert the Video and/or View modes.

Display Resolution

A computer monitor (display) is measured in pixels, little squares that are the basic component of a computer graphic. According to www.w3schools.com, the trend in monitor display resolution is higher than 1024 x 768 pixels. If a monitor is set to show more pixels, it is known as increasing the resolution. At a higher resolution, graphics and text look sharper, but smaller. The fewer pixels, the lower the resolution and the larger the screen elements appear.

If your computer is set to a high resolution (such as 1280 x 1024) when you record screen captures using Articulate Storyline, a learner viewing your published lesson on a display using a lower display resolution (such as 1024 x 768) may be forced to scroll significantly to see the action you recorded. Prior to recording screen actions, you should set your computer display to the same resolution (or perhaps a slightly lower resolution) than you expect your learners to be using. Of course, that doesn't mean that you should set the resolution so low that your display looks terrible—use your best judgment. If you are creating eLearning lessons for internal employees, your corporate IT department likely knows the typical display size and resolution used on computers in your organization. If your lessons are intended for the public at large, you need to make a best guess as to the typical display resolution your customers will be using. Storyline allows you to set the learner's browser size when viewing your published lesson to either **Display at user's current browser size**, **Resize browser to optimal size**, or **Resize browser to fill screen**.

Recording Frame

The Recording Frame is not the same as Display Resolution (the two settings are often confused). The Display Resolution is controlled via your computer's Display settings. In contrast, the Recording Frame is set from within Storyline and is the physical amount of the screen that you will be capturing during the recording process.

Rehearsals

Prior to recording screen actions, you'll need to write a step-by-step script. Then you'll need to rehearse the script to ensure its accuracy. Here's the scenario for the recording you are about to create: you have been hired to create an eLearning course that demonstrates the process of using a credit score estimator.

Here is a sample script showing the kind of detailed, step-by-step instructions you need to create or receive from a SME.

Dear Storyline developer, you're going to demonstrate how easy it is to use our Credit Score Estimator by using its various sliders and tools. In this instance, you'll be getting a credit score for someone named Biff Bifferson (who isn't going to fare so well). Thanks. Your pal, the Subject Matter Expert.

First things first: open the calculator by visiting iconlogic.com/creditscore/calculators/score/index.html.

1. From the "When was the last negative item on your credit score" area, drag the slider to 6 months (the third tick mark from the left).

2. From the "How many of the following accounts" area, select four credit cards.

3. Select two mortgages.

4. From the "Retail Finance" area, select the fifth shopping cart.

5. From the "Auto Loans" area, select three cars.

6. From the "Student Loan" area, select the first one.

7. From the "Other Loans" area, select two.

8. From the "Add up all the credit limits" area, drag the slider right to $70,000.

9. From the "Add up all the most recent" area, drag the slide right to $63,000.

10. From the "How many times have you applied" area, drag the slider right to 5.

11. From the When did you first open your oldest area, drag the slide right to 8 years.

12. Click the "Calculate My Credit Score" button.

13. At this point you can stop the recording process.

The script sounds simple. However, you will not know what kind of trouble you are going to get into unless you rehearse the script prior to recording the process with Storyline. Let's go ahead and run a rehearsal, just as if you were a big-time movie director and you are in charge of a blockbuster movie.

Places everyone... and quiet on the set...

Student Activity: Rehearse a Script

1. Minimize Storyline. (You will be using a web browser during the next few steps.)

2. Open the credit score calculator.

   ❑ using a web browser, open the following web page:
   iconlogic.com/creditscore/calculators/score/index.html

3. Rehearse the script.

   ❑ from the **When was the last negative item on your credit score** area, drag the slider to **6 months** (the third tick mark from the left)

   ❑ from the **How many of the following accounts** area, select **four** credit cards

   ❑ select **two mortgages**

   ❑ from the **Retail Finance** area, select the **fifth** shopping cart

   ❑ from the **Auto Loans** area, select **three cars**

   ❑ from the **Student Loan** area, select the **first one**

   ❑ from the **Other Loans** area, select **two**

   ❑ from the **Add up all the credit limits** area, drag the slider right to **$70,000**

   ❑ from the **Add up all the most recent** area, drag the slider right to **$63,000**

   ❑ from the **How many times have you applied** area, drag the slider right to **5**

   ❑ from the **When did you first open your oldest** area, drag the slider right to **8** years

   ❑ click the **Calculate My Credit Score** button

   ❑ press [**escape**] on your keyboard (even though Storyline isn't currently recording, it's a good idea to practice the process of stopping the recording)

4. Keep the Credit Score Estimator window open in your web browser (you'll be recording the application soon).

5. Switch back to Storyline.

Student Activity: Record a Video

1. Using Storyline, open the **RecordMe** project from the Storyline360Data folder.

2. Ensure that you are working in Story View.

3. Open and resize the Recording Frame.

   ❏ select the **Slides** tab on the Ribbon, and then click **Record Screen**

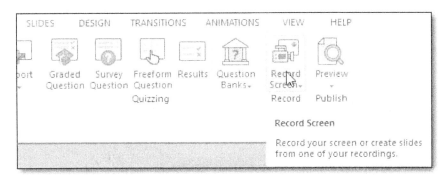

The Recording Frame appears in the middle of screen. At this point, you can resize the Recording Frame so that it encompasses the Credit Score Estimator tool, or you can resize the browser window so it fits within the Recording Frame.

   ❏ resize both the **Recording Frame** and the **Credit Score Estimator** so that your screen is similar to the image below

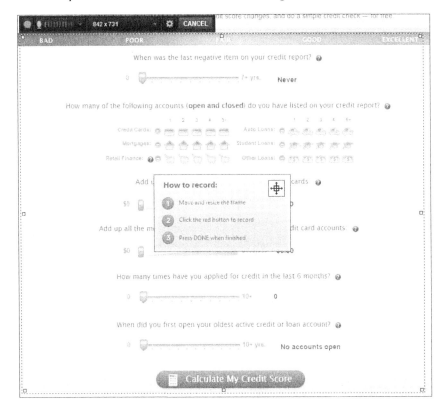

4. Edit Storyline's Recording settings.

    ❏ from the Recording control panel, click **Settings** (the gear icon to the left of Cancel)

The Screen Recording dialog box opens.

❏ if necessary, deselect **Microphone**

Often times the person who records the screen actions is not the voiceover talent. Also, if you record your voice while recording the screen actions, you will likely record more voiceover gaffes. The ideal workflow will be to record screen actions without recording the voiceover and inserting the voiceover audio files you receive from the voiceover talent later. (You learned how to insert audio on page 138.)

5. Observe the Stop recording shortcut.

    ❏ from the **Shortcuts** area, confirm that **Escape** is the default **Stop recording** key

When you are finished with the Recording process, pressing [Escape] on your keyboard forces Storyline to stop recording your screen actions.

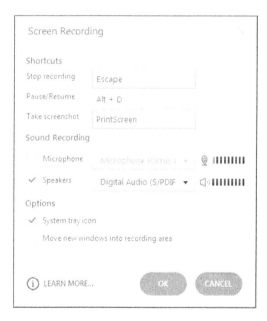

❏ click the **OK** button

6. Record a video.

    ❏ **refresh** the browser window (to reset the calculator) and then click the **Record** button

After an initial countdown, nothing seems to happening. However, Storyline is recording.

☐ from the **When was the last negative item on your credit score** area, drag the slider to **6 months** (the third tick mark from the left)

☐ from the **How many of the following accounts** area, select **four** credit cards

☐ select **two mortgages**

☐ from the **Retail Finance** area, select the **fifth** shopping cart

☐ from the **Auto Loans** area, select **three cars**

☐ from the **Student Loan** area, select the **first one**

☐ from the **Other Loans** area, select **two**

☐ from the **Add up all the credit limits** area, drag the slider right to **$70,000**

☐ from the **Add up all the most recent** area, drag the slider right to **$63,000**

☐ from the **How many times have you applied** area, drag the slider right to **5**

☐ from the **When did you first open your oldest** area, drag the slider right to **8** years

☐ click the **Calculate My Credit Score** button

☐ stop the recording process by pressing [**escape**] on your keyboard

Once you stop the recording process, the Insert Slides dialog box opens. You have created a single recording that can be used in four different ways: Video Mode, View Mode, Try Mode, and Test Mode. You'll be using the Video Mode in your project.

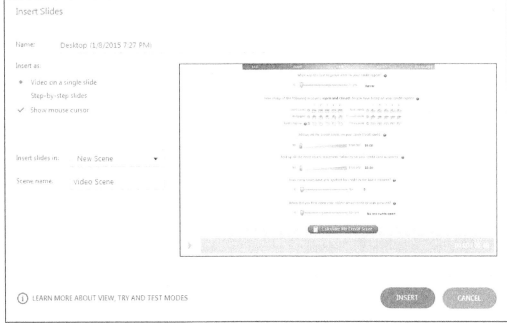

7. Preview the video.

❑ with the Insert Slides dialog box open, click the **Play** button just beneath the video to see the steps that you recorded

8. Insert the video.

❑ with the Insert Slides dialog box still open, change the name to **Credit Score Estimator**

❑ from the **Insert as** area, ensure that **Video on a single slide** is selected

❑ ensure that **Show mouse cursor** is selected

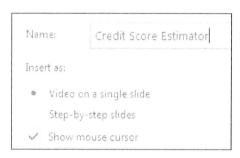

❑ from the **Insert slides in** drop-down menu, choose **4 Lightbox**

❑ click the **Insert** button

The video is inserted in the Lightbox scene. There is a placeholder slide in the scene that you'll need to delete. You'll also update a Trigger to ensure that the video appears in the Lightbox.

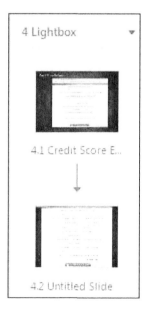

9. Delete a slide.

    ❏ right-click slide **4.1** and choose **Delete**

    ❏ click the **Yes** button

10. Name a slide.

    ❏ select slide **4.1**

    ❏ double-click the words **Untitled Slide**

    ❏ change the slide's name to **Credit Score Calculator**

11. Update a Trigger.

    ❏ open slide **2.4**

    ❏ on the **Triggers** panel, **Lightbox slide** trigger, click the word **unassigned**

    ❏ choose **4.1 Credit Score Calculator**

    Lightbox 4.1 Credit Score Calculator
    When the user clicks

12. Preview the project.

13. Jump to the **Credit Score Resources** slide and click the text in the middle of the screen.

    You should be on the Lightbox slide and see the video you created of the Credit Score Calculator.

14. Close the Preview.

15. Close the slide.

16. Save and close the project.

Player Settings

You will soon be publishing your eLearning project. Prior to publishing, you can customize the **Player** (the skin that surrounds your lesson). When customizing the Player, you can add branding (including your logo, corporate colors, and language), and you can elect to include a Menu, Glossary, and even a Resources area.

Student Activity: Edit Player Properties

1. Open the **PublishMe** project from the Storyline360Data folder.

2. Open the Player Properties dialog box.

   ❐ select the **Home** tab on the Ribbon

   ❐ from the **Publish** group, click **Player**

3. Edit the Player Tabs.

   ❐ from the top left of the dialog box, click **Features**

   ❐ from the **Player Tabs** area, deselect **Resources**

   The Resources shown in the Preview at the right. go away.

   ❐ from the **Sidebar** area, ensure that **Menu** and **Notes** are selected

   ❐ ensure that **Glossary** is deselected

   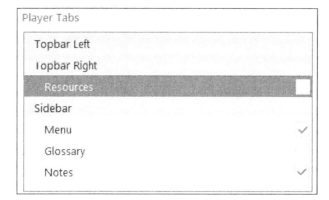

4. Add a Title.

   ❏ from the **Features** area, ensure **Title** is selected

   ❏ change the **Title** to **Credit Score eCoach**

   ❏ from the **Sidebar** drop-down menu, ensure that **On Left** is selected

5. Enable the Seekbar.

   ❏ from the **Controls** area, ensure that **Volume** is selected

   ❏ ensure that **Search** is deselected

   ❏ select **Seekbar**

   The Search option allows learners to find text within the menu or on any slide. The Seekbar allows learners to see how far they have advanced in any slide. It also allows the learner to fast-forward or rewind a slide.

   ❏ from the **Seekbar** drop-down menu, ensure that **Allow user to drag seekbar** is selected

6. Add a logo.

   ❏ from the **Controls** area, select **Logo**

   ❏ click the link **Click to add a logo**

   ❏ from the **Storyline360Data** folder, open **images_animation**

   ❏ open **creditScore-logo**

7. Customize the Menu.

   ❏ from the top of the dialog box, click **Menu**

   ❏ from Scene 2, double-click **Hello: %learnerName%**

❏ change the text to **Calculate Your Credit Score Range**

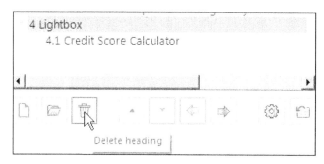

2 Credit eCoach
        2.1 Calculate Your Credit Score Range

❏ from **Scene 4**, select **4 Lightbox**
❏ from the bottom of the dialog box, click **Delete heading**

4 Lightbox
        4.1 Credit Score Calculator

Delete heading

❏ click the **Remove** button

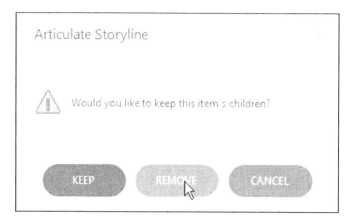

Articulate Storyline

⚠ Would you like to keep this item's children?

KEEP   REMOVE   CANCEL

Your menu should look like the picture below.

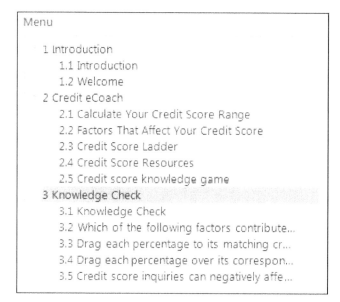

Menu

    1 Introduction
        1.1 Introduction
        1.2 Welcome
    2 Credit eCoach
        2.1 Calculate Your Credit Score Range
        2.2 Factors That Affect Your Credit Score
        2.3 Credit Score Ladder
        2.4 Credit Score Resources
        2.5 Credit score knowledge game
    3 Knowledge Check
        3.1 Knowledge Check
        3.2 Which of the following factors contribute...
        3.3 Drag each percentage to its matching cr...
        3.4 Drag each percentage over its correspon...
        3.5 Credit score inquiries can negatively affe...

8. Edit the Color scheme.

❏ from the top of the dialog box, click **Colors & Effects**

❏ from the **Color scheme** drop-down menu, choose **Black**

9. Save the changes to the Player Properties.

❏ from the top of the dialog box, click **Current Player** and choose **Save as**

The Player Name dialog box opens.

❏ change the name to **Credit Score Player**

☐ click the **OK** button

☐ click the **OK** button

10. Save your work.

11. Preview the Entire Project.

    The changes you made to the Player are evident as you move through the lesson.

12. Close the Preview.

Student Activity: Reorder Slides and Edit Triggers

1. Ensure that the PublishMe project is still open.

2. Ensure that you are in Story View.

3. Reorder slides.

   ❏ in the **Introduction** scene, drag slide **1.1** after slide **1.2**

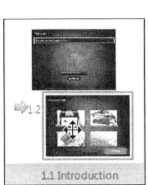 

Now that you've reordered the slides, you need to ensure that the navigation continues to work as expected. Slide to slide navigation is easy to control via the Triggers panel.

4. Edit Triggers.

   ❏ select slide **1.1** (there is no need to open the slide)

   ❏ on the **Triggers** panel, under **Button 1**, click the words **Jump to 2.1 Hello:**

   ❏ choose **1.2 Introduction**

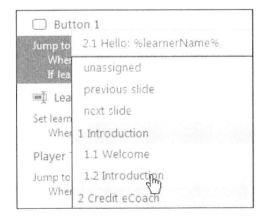

5. Remove Slide navigation controls.

☐ select slide **1.1** (there is still no need to open the slide)

☐ on the **Slide Properties** panel, **Slide navigation and gestures** area, deselect **Prev**

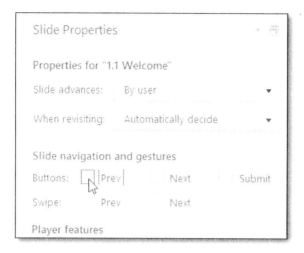

Slide Navigation Confidence Check

1. Select slide **1.2** and, on the **Triggers** panel, ensure that the Trigger for the Continue button jumps to **2.1 Hello:**.

2. Still working on slide **1.2**, use the Slide Properties panel to add a **Prev** control for Slide navigation and gestures.

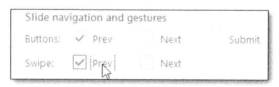

3. Select slide **2.5** (the Credit score knowledge game).

4. On the **Triggers** panel, **Player Triggers** area, change the **Jump to next slide** to Jump to slide **3.1**

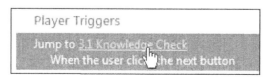

5. Open slide **2.1** (Hello: %learnerName).

6. Click the **Insert** tab on the Ribbon and, from the **Media** area, click **Web Object**.

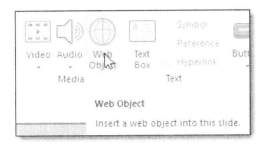

A Web Object gives you a way to add live web content to your project. For instance, you added a demonstration video of the Credit Score Calculator to your project earlier. But if you want learners to actually use the calculator, the web object you are adding now will take learners directly to the tool.

7. On the Insert Web Object dialog, enter the following web address: **http://www.iconlogic.com/creditscore/calculators/score/index.html**

8. From the **How do you want to display this web object?** area, ensure that **Display in slide** is selected.

9. Resize and position the web object so your screen is similar to the image below.

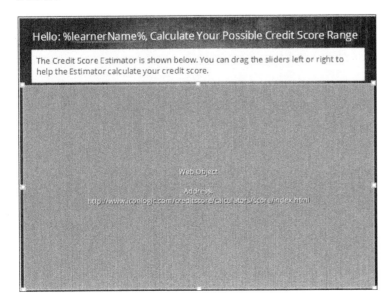

10. Open slide **2.3**.

When learner's click each of the green rectangles, they'll get feedback right beside the rectangle in the form of thumbs up if the factor is good for their credit; they'll get thumbs down if it's bad. In addition to a thumbs up or thumbs down, you're going to change the character's expression. The character will smile if the factor is good (the second and third rectangles) and frown if it's bad (the first and fourth factors).

11. Select the **High Debt to Credit Ratio** rectangle. (Remember, this factor is bad so the character should appear stressed.)

12. On the Trigger panel, click **Create a new trigger.**

13. Set the **Action** to **Change state of**.

14. Set the **On Object** to **Character 1**.

15. Set the **To State** to **Stressed**.

16. Set the **When** to **User clicks**.

17. Set the Object to **Rectangle 1**.

18. Select the **Consolidate Debt** rectangle. (This factor is good, so the character should appear to be happy.)

19. On the Trigger panel, click **Create a new trigger.**

20. Set the **Action** to **Change state of**.

21. Set the **On Object** to **Character 1**.

22. Set the **To State** to **Happy**.

23. Set the **When** to **User clicks**.

24. Set the Object to **Rectangle 2**.

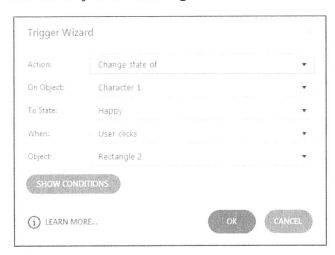

25. Repeat the steps for the **Pay On Time** rectangle (using **Happy** as the To State).

26. Repeat the steps for the Close Zero Balance Cards (using **Stressed** as the To State).

27. Preview the project.

    The first slide you should see is the video introducing the lesson. After that, you should be prompted to enter your name. After clicking Continue, you should jump to the lesson overview and then continue through the lesson.

    When you get to the web object that you just added, you'll be alerted that it will not work while you are previewing. No worries, the object will work correctly once you publish the lesson later.

    When you get to the Credit Score Ladder, clicking the factors will make the character look either happy or stressed. (The character isn't very large, so you'll have to look closely.)

    There's a problem that needs your attention: After you take the quiz (slide 3.6), notice that there is a Next button on the Quiz Results slide that doesn't serve any purpose. You need to disable the Next button on the slide.

28. Close the preview and select slide **3.6**.

29. On the Slide Properties panel, deselect **Next** from both the **Buttons** and **Swipe** areas.

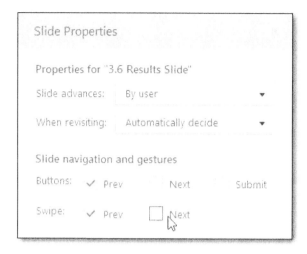

30. Preview the project again and notice when you complete the quiz that the quiz results slide no longer has a Next button.

31. Close the Preview.

32. Save your work (keep the project open for the next activity).

Publishing

Publishing in Storyline takes your source content and outputs it into a format that can be consumed (viewed) by the learner. Currently, the most common way to publish a Storyline project is as a Flash SWF and HTML5, an excellent solution allowing you to reach the widest possible audience. Your learners do **not** need Storyline installed on their computer to view your published content, but they do need a modern web browser or mobile device. The Flash version of your published lesson will automatically open if your learner is using a device that supports Flash; otherwise, the learner will automatically be served the HTML5 version.

In addition to publishing for the Web, you can also publish your Storyline project for use in a standard Learning Management System (LMS), upload your content to Articulate Online (Articulate's LMS), burn your lesson to a CD, and create handouts of your lesson in Microsoft Word.

Student Activity: Publish Course Content

1. Ensure that the **PublishMe** project is still open. (As an alternative to publishing the PublishMe project, you can also open and work with the Finished_CreditScore_eCoach.story project.)

2. Display the Publish dialog box.

   ☐ choose **File > Publish**

3. Add Project Info.

   ☐ from the left side of the dialog box, ensure that **Web** is selected

   ☐ from the **Title** area, click the **Browse** button (the three dots)

   The Project Info. dialog box opens.

   ☐ change the Title to **Credit eCoach**

Title:	Credit eCoach

   ☐ in the **Author** field, add yourself as the Author

   ☐ in the **Email** field, add your email

   ☐ in the **Website** field, add your corporate or personal website URL

Author:	Biff Bifferson
Email:	biff@supersimplisticsolutions.com
Website:	http://www.supersimplisticsolutions.com

   ☐ click the **OK** button to return to the Publish dialog box

4. Specify a Publish destination.

❏ to the right of **Folder**, click the **Browse** button

❏ open the **Storyline360Data** folder and then open the **published_projects** folder

❏ click the **Select Folder** button

5. Ensure that you are Publishing first for HTML5 and then Flash.

❏ from the **Properties** area, **Formats**, click **Flash with HTML 5 fallback**

The Publish Formats dialog box opens. By default, your published project will use Flash output first and use HTML 5 output if the learner's device does not support Flash. Instead, you want the output to use HTML5 by default, and Flash if HTML5 is not supported.

❏ drag the **Publish As** slider **left** to **HTML5/Flash**

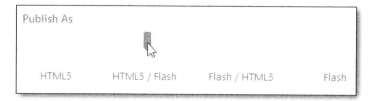

❏ ensure that **Use Articulate Mobile Player for iOS or Android** is **selected**

❏ deselect **Allow downloading for offline viewing**

Allowing your lesson to be downloaded for offline viewing is a double-edged sword. If you allow this option, mobile learners will be able to consume your content even when not online. However, if your lesson needs to be tracked or resides within a Learning Management System, allowing for offline viewing could cause reporting issues (including reporting inaccuracies).

❑ click the **OK** button to return to the Publish dialog box

❑ click the **Publish** button

Once the project has been published, the Publish Successful dialog box opens. From here you can view the published lesson, FTP the published assets to a web server, zip the assets, or view the HTML5 version of the published lesson.

❑ click the **View Project** button

The lesson opens in your default web browser. Congratulations, you are now a published eLearning author!

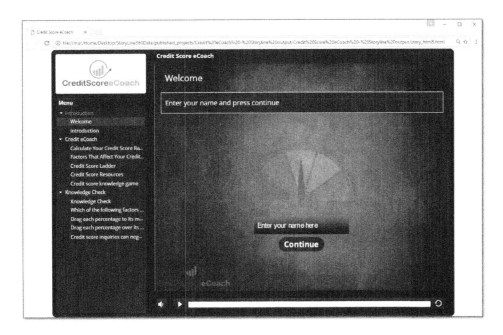

6. Close the browser window and return to Storyline. (The Publish Successful dialog box should still be open.)

7. Observe the Published files.

    ☐ on the **Publish Successful** dialog box, click **Open**

    The Storyline output folder opens. The story.html file is the start (home) page. This is the file that your learner will need access to when starting the lesson. Story_html5 is the HTML5 version of the lesson; story_flash.html is the Flash version of the lesson. All of the files in this folder need to be uploaded to your web server together. You should never rename any of the files or change the folder structure (doing so will likely result in the lesson not playing correctly if all).

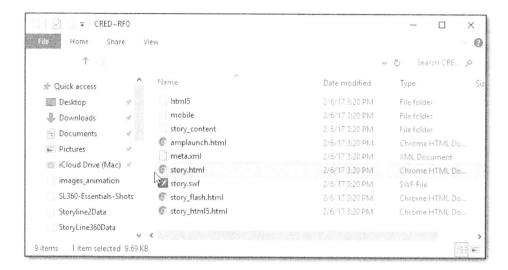

8. Close the window and return to Storyline.

9. Close the Publish Successful dialog box.

Publish Confidence Check

1. Still working in the PublishMe project, open the Publish dialog box.

2. From the list of options at the left, click **Word**.

3. Change the **Screenshot size** to **Large** and Publish the output to the **Storyline360Data/published_projects** folder.

4. When finished publishing, **View the Document**.

   You can use this version of your lesson as handouts to support your eLearning course.

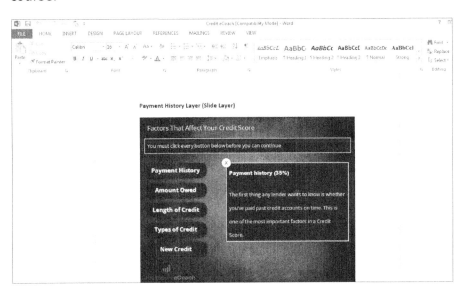

5. Close the Word document.

6. Save and close the Storyline project.

Notes

Index

H
Handouts, 203
Helvetica, 10
Hide Player Buttons, 100
Hide slide objects, 58
Hide Slide Player
    Buttons, 100
Home tab, 31
Hotspots, 111
How Software Updates Affect
    This Book, ix
HTML5, 3, 203

I
Icons, 3
Illustrations, 3
Images, 63
    GIF, 63
    JPEG, 63
Input, 92
Insert Layout, 42
Insert Web Object, 199
Integration with Articulate
    Review for Stakeholder
    Reviews, 3
Interactive
    Objects, 80, 81, 92
Interface, Storyline, 16
Internal margin, 56

K
Keep Source Formatting, 54

L
Label, 80
Label and Name a button, 81
Layers, 87
Learners with disabilities, 4
Learning Management
    System, 203, 205
Lightbox, 111
Line Spacing, 60
Lists, 57
LMS, 203
Logo, Add to Player, 193
L-Shape, 70

M
Manage project
    variables, 125
Master Layout group, 42
Master Slides, 36
Match column, 174
Matching Drag-and-Drop
    Slide, 173
Media group, 138
Menu, Customize, 193
Microphone, 188
Microphone placement, 146
Microphone technique, 146
Microsoft, 11

Microsoft PowerPoint, 4
Microsoft Word, 203
MPEG Audio Layer III, 138
Multiple Choice Slide, 168

N
Name, 80
Name scenes, 32
Narration Script, 148
New Content Master
    Slides, 42
New Project, Create, 30
New Scene, 31
New Slides, 40
Next, 100
Notes, 146, 148

O
On Condition, 129
Open a project, 17

P
Palatino, 10
Panels, 19
Passing Score, 180
Paste content from Word
    into Storyline, 57
Paste Options, 57
Pasting
    Destination Theme, 54
    Keep Source
        Formatting, 54
    Text Only, 54
Peek, 2
Personas, Fonts, 11
Photographic Character, 74
Pictures, 63
Pixels, 184
Placeholders, 42
Planning eLearning
    Projects, 4
Play Audio, 133
Player, 113
Player Properties, 192
Point value, 170
Points area, 170
Popular Fonts, 10
Position on slide, 68
PowerPoint Integration, 48
Presenter, 2
Preso, 2
Prev, 100, 198
Preview, 25
Preview a project, 25
Publish, 205
Publish destination, 204
Publish Successful dialog
    box, 206
Published files., 206
Publishing, 203
Push, 164

Q
Questions, 169
Quiz Result Slide, 179
Quiz Slides, 168
Quizzing, 168, 173, 175, 17
    9

R
Random bars, 151
Readability of Fonts, 9
Recent area, 18
Recent tab, 18
Record a Video, 187
Record button, 188
Record Mic, 148
Record Screen, 187
Record Your Screen, 187
Recording, 184
Recording control panel, 188
Recording Frame, 184
Recording Size, 184
Red flag in the upper left of a
    scene, 31
Redock All Windows, 24
Rehearsals, 146, 185
Reorder Slides, 197
Replay 360, 2
Reset Don't Show Again
    Prompts, 27
Reset from Story, 113
Reset the Player Menu, 113
Reset the player menu, 113
Resize browser to fill
    screen, 184
Resize browser to optimal
    size, 184
Resolution, 184
Resolution and Recording
    Size, 16, 30, 47, 51, 80,
    96, 116, 138, 168
Responsive Playback
    options, 26
Result Slide Properties, 179
Result Tools Design tab, 180
Ribbon, 31
Rise, 2
Rotation, 71

S
Sample Script, 12
Sample Storyboard, 13
Sans Serif, 9
Scenes, 19, 30
Scenes group, 31
Screen Captures, 184
Screenshot size, 207
Scripts, 12
Scripts in Paragraph
    Format, 12
Scripts in Table Format, 12
Seekbar, 193

Notes

Printed in Great Britain
by Amazon